The Man i Love

KILLED ME

○ ○ ○

NOVELLA

AUTHOR

Cláudia Cassoma

www.claudiacassoma.com

TITLE

The Man i Love Killed Me

IMAGE ON THE COVER

Efes Kitap

GRAPHIC COMPOSITION

Cláudia Cassoma / Kujikula™

PUBLISHER

Kujikula™

www.kujikula.com

info@kujikula.com

ISBN (paperback): 978-1-7348776-0-1
ISBN (hardcover): 979-8-9863273-4-1

2nd Edition — June 15, 2022
1st Edition — June 15, 2020

The Man i Love

KILLED ME

○ ○ ○

CLÁUDIA CASSOMA

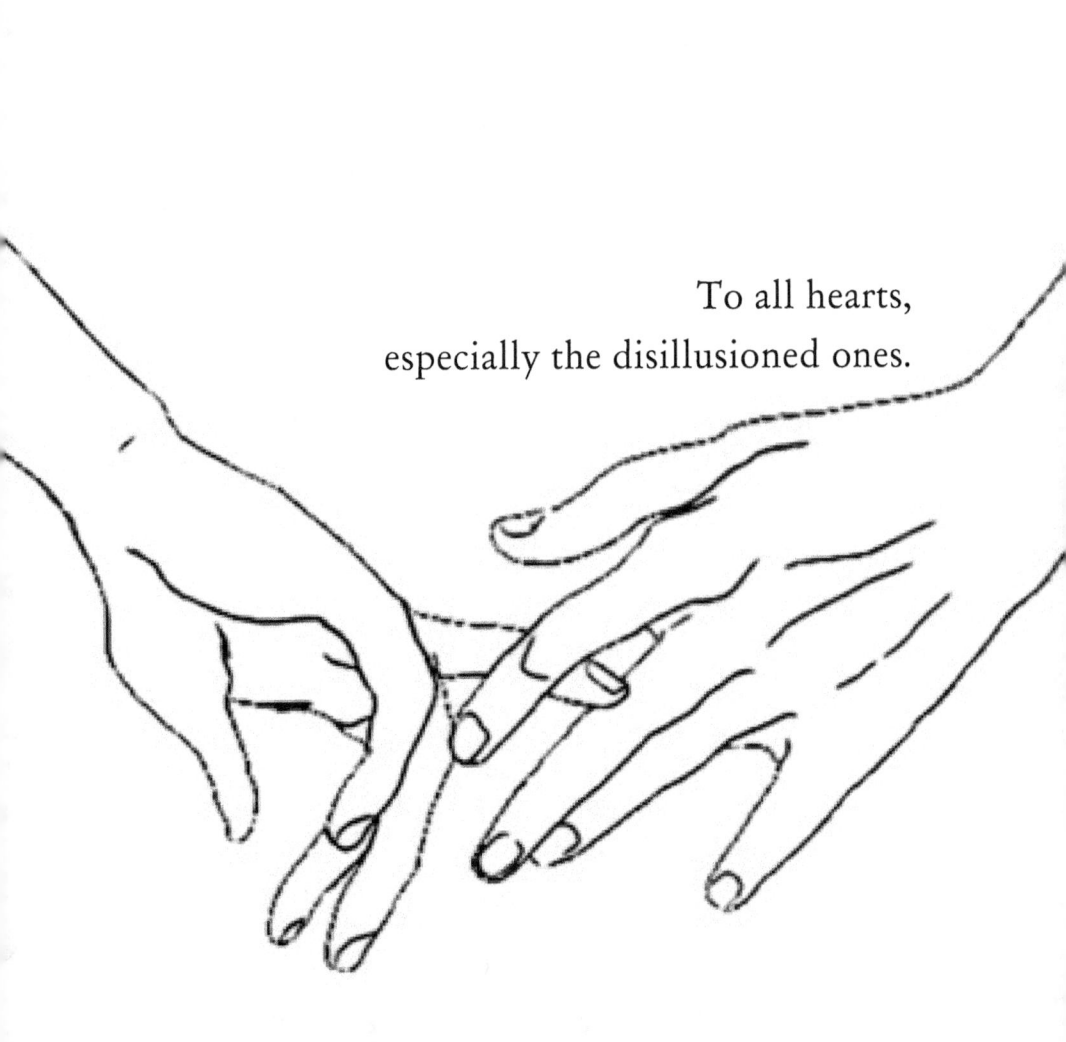

To all hearts,
especially the disillusioned ones.

you'll know it's true love
when you find yourself
with a bowl of ice cream
sprinkled with tears

Four seasons had already passed since we last spoke. Still time purged absolutely nothing. The trees didn't have the shine of always. And there was no more snow to shovel. The path was numb. Leaves and flowers left the ground fearing the end of spring. The waves were no longer dancing on top of the sea, neither was the sun shining for his Mother. Though sometimes i could watch the rain fall, the garden was more malnourished than ever. Life as we knew it felt awfully gray. i saw no children playing under the frigid sky-water of May, no snowman in January, and those days of June were nothing like the previous ones. i was convinced that we had a long way ahead of us, but that too turned out to be wild frenzy.

We had spent a lot of time talking – and the truth i felt, consumed me more than the anguish of losing Him. i read all the magazines, watched long movies while eating ice-cream and sitting on popcorn. i even rushed into new kisses. But nothing worked. i was still just pain.

Since nature already had her own rain, i looked for other places to keep the salt fleeing my eyes. The sharp sheets of water refused to hide my heartbreak. i considered throwing our memories on fire. Keep the truth at the end of my tears; and smile to hide my fears. Like newly singles in romantic comedies, i'd simply restart: drink, dress up and go dancing. My strength would've been clear as a day. i was strong enough. i too could move on and find another. i wore a smile to deceive anyone. And maybe it did. But, in the wake of a new season, to annul the bright outlook, i was found with nothing but the messages we exchanged, and a far-reaching call history filled with outgoings.

i had been there. i knew the feeling very well. Yet i could not bring myself to believe. Playing a part in that surreal affair felt too hard to endure. Completely unknown to my senses.

My eyes had already distended from the long rivers i cried. My frame went out through my skin – clear as my tears. Worse still, i found myself unable to rescue summer. To check my reasons. To know my wits. To all who saw, my life was messier than the picture i had of His room. The one dreamt on one of the good old days — back when a call nourished our flames:

A full-size bed in the center, encircled by pallid walls and a brown closet not far from the white door. Mounts of vestures blending His moisture in corners everywhere. That i knew about His room. i knew Him very well. He was His most untidy self with a piercing tone on His voice. The waves reached my ears like a well-rehearsed choir in the feel of a song.

"Wanna organize my things?" – He pled.

He might've been playing, but, by then, i already was in my lacy apron with matching gloves. When He rang those words on my ears; when He took the risk, unaware of my thirst; The Man i Love asked a question that could've easily been perceived as offensive. But i didn't.

He didn't know i would take any chance to be with Him between four walls. i would've loved to make them perspire, crack, and even fall due to my piercing cries. My eyes closed would be the peak of our pleasure, the reach of our joy, and way more than brisk gratification.

He would have no doubt about the truths in my heart. Even from His point-of-view, i would be truly on. He would know. My groans would be everything. The tightest screams of my lungs would ring loud enough to deafen. Birds would have no other choice but to find far away heavens to nest. At last, my finishing squeals would paralyze Him – The Man i Love.

If only i was there or He was here.

Either way, glasses and bottles would've been dispensed because our fire would have been more than alight. No wine would incite more than our bare desires. But for all that, in every pixel of my deepest cravings, i was alone.

"What would i get in return?" – i teased.

Before He attempted to escape His own snare, voiding the question with useless tales, i gave Him my conditions for accepting that outmoded proposal. The Man i Love saw just how well the apron fitted and where the gloves would end up at the end of the night. He knew:

His arms around me like heat of summer. It was spring deep bellow the equator. And when winter overwhelmed, fall was there to ease. Somehow, He was warmer and seemed stronger. We moved our heads like starving snakes. We kissed like the world was ending.

With His hands narrowed around my waist, sucking the life out of me, The Man i Love made me ready. i was there; and i stayed. Until a light-footed silence-breaker swapped those truths with deceiving smiles and loud silences.

My ears didn't mind the hit, nor wailed my body for rolling all over the bed we once shared. When the phone broiled, i simply put it elsewhere. When my hands tired, i wheeled.

We had our bodies involved in a restless tussle anent the level they should've reached. Had no labels, made no real plans; everything looked far too novelistic. All we knew about the season was that it felt suitable for brown leather balls with pointy ends — His favorites!

The screams of pride behind every field goal were His fuel. In turn, my nights heated. In spite the lack of space in His car, He buried my assets under the life of His tall frame. After each game, The Man i Love made me His rave.

Loss of breath. Rise of appetite. Nirvana! Best moments of our lives. And we had lots of them. The Man i Love knew just how much i waited for our caloric transfusions; that is why He always gave us the attention we deserved.

Once connected, we shared dreams, we converted lies and lived fully. All in that twin bed made nowhere gracious. There, we linked the corners of our bodies like a meant-to-be puzzle. The meeting of my eyelids filled Him. On the springs of that old mattress we went deep into what we were. Overwhelmed with blinding zeal, we both embarked on a long ravishing trip. A memorable craze. My eyes' quivering was the thrill of the game. Our game! We floated on a field of intense touchdowns.

The tall, wide figure of His, played ball like it was the solution for everything. i'd never seen His flea flicks or legendary fumbles, but they were in our talks. Can't remember flowers or chocolate, nor nights coiled in prolonged hugs, but i knew how much he loved football.

We had no need for dim and trivial pet-names. We didn't build seemingly perfect stories. Never. We were nothing like the other twosomes. Ours was always just ours: not too contradicting, but quite daring. Fused with our own rules and spared by a dreamlike romance.

"I like touching what's mine," He affirm.

Had He any idea of that blow? Did He know it would send me to a state of madness?

"If you were mine, I would go through every single inch of you" – He preceded to say.

i wasn't ready! My mouth shut, my eyes widened, my body bristled and froze. All while welcoming a forever moment with The Man i Love. He was fervent, exact, and of few words.

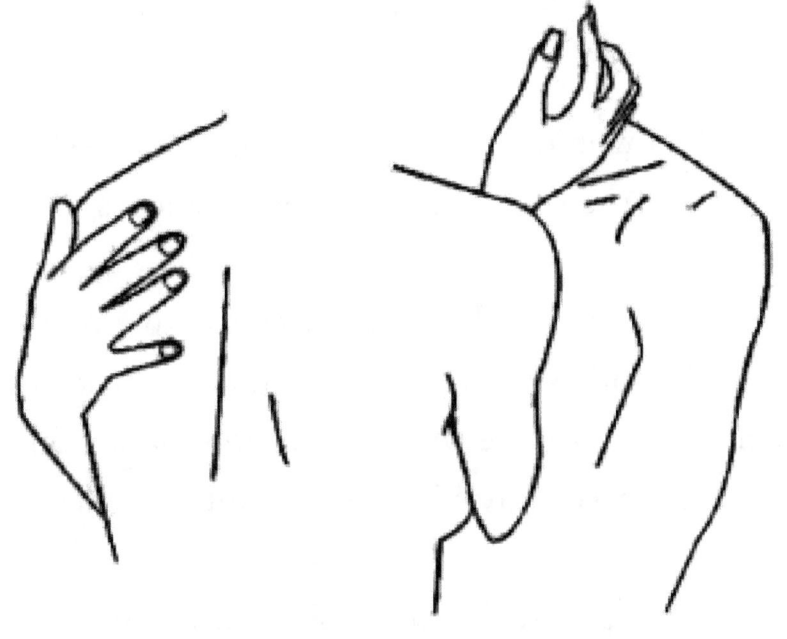

Had He realized the unrest of my heart, He would watch His mouth, even when just talking game. As He forced a silence in the room, gazed at my eyes and uttered those lines, i purpled. My mind couldn't help but get lost in anticipation. Only, like buffer, almost at the same second, He stuck His nose on my frenzies.

"I would watch my p.d.a, of course" – He vowed. And then, there was a wink and a smile.

It was as if He felt the need to explain His words, and assert His desires. Like, somehow, there was pleasure wrapped around shame. But i never craved anything else, i wanted the dare.

"In public?" – my teased smile said it all.

"Absolutely! I would have my hands at your ends; I'd take you by the depth of your waist; and I'd play with you like Super Bowl was all year long", The Man i Love concluded.

He never heard me say the words, still, He knew i was just the woman for that: to stop, to close my eyes, to give up control, and to be overtaken. i loved nothing but being touched, and well touched. He knew how. So, in public or by ourselves – He was very welcome indeed.

There we were: walking down the mall hall holding hands, attaching them like they were meant to be connected. i would spread my shyness like always, saying 'i love you' with just a smile and 'i want you' with a passionate chomp on my bottom lip. And, in spite of His deep desire to avoid cliché, He would look at me, fondle my face, and embed a kiss between my brows making me sprout a rainbow from my cheeks. On the shade of a bright night, as we secured a filled popcorn-holder between our sits, i'd realize the moment before us. The instant we would make the most of our free-will. i would call a halt to my stargazing and He'd no longer avoid His long-burning desires.

In the cuddle of The Man i Love, i would always carry superior brightness, even when my wrinkles were outed. But for all that, His wounds would always be my enduring distress.

There was a time He deprived me of one of the habitual calls. He got out of work late and embarked on a solo commute. In the guise of my pupils, His exhaustion became evident as quick as a wink. On that dark rainy day, right before He got into the three-ninety-five intersection, a Lamborghini Asterion came printing its all-season tires under another car's bonnet, dragging the car of The Man i Love with it. Nobody knew exactly how that guy got his car to visit the Nissan Frontier's bottom, and neither did i. In any case, the only thing that mattered was having The Man i Love out of that testosterone-spilling scene and with me.

Had He not blinked, had the lights not been red, had somebody pressed their hooter hard enough, much would have been avoided.

Most importantly, had The Man i Love called me before starting His car as He had always done, i would not have this awful story to tell.

"I fell asleep for a second, and someone was committed to, literally, slap me out of it."

My body was obviously much more marked by anxiety than His. He always felt the need to display some unreasonable strength despite His pains and fears. i didn't fully understand, but often blamed it on some sort of societal pressure. When finally the muscles of The Man i Love weakened, as His failed attempt to fake composure, He tried to quickly turn things into a sobersided joke. But i knew.

i surely remember the few occasions He discussed His old man. Every time He spilled out their shared-moments, i would feel tears knocking down His eyes with great urgency. As expected, He would throw a smile in the air like it was the easiest thing He had just done. Good thing, a few of them would inevitably reach the cunning mountains of His glorious round face. The Man i Love would ensure me that He could never be the kind of father that just left. On times He tried His father's shoes, He wore a relief that wrapped Him with pride:

"By grabbing his little hand, assuring that all fingers were protected; by taking his small yet season-ready feet to the park; and, by shooting the moon, we would play ball 'til the sun went down. Moments after that, with our shirts still muddy, we'd go for ice cream--" His dream.

i have always admired a man untroubled by his tears. He who does not fear the suffering, but let it mend. Like his next day depended on it, spurs the release of all the embodied pain. i've absolutely always had the strongest feeling towards a human that allowed himself to be just that – a being all-out with ups and downs.

i still have the photos from when my father cried. My nana had just given her last sigh and he too realized that there was nothing else to be done. He tried quite stiffly – if i may add – to keep his beautiful-smoky smile intact; but for my comfort, even the strongest person feels when a sword is gored deep into his heart.

i saw my father's pain leave his eyes in a rush. For the very first time, the square-cloth-napkin that practically lived in his pocket was put to use. From a painful distance, i watched as it took a course to his eyes. And, on its way back, it looked as if it had just been dumped into a large wet bucket and never squeezed. My heart grew strained. It was there i understood manhood. It was there that i saw a whole-man.

The Man i Love was the one long carried far down in my unvoiced desires. Perfect in His imperfections; sensitive, shredded, and well-spirited. So, my search ended right away. i had found the last. And i knew it! He was all over.

i had my mind laden with moments of His. My past was nothing but a past. A life gone. My present was short when we talked, and so long when we didn't. He was all over. i did know it!

On a night the sky exposed all her stars—planted at my balcony with the phone glued to my ear—apparently on a spur of the moment, as i was struck by the blazing rays of His voice, The Man i Love validated one of my illusions:

"I would sing for you every day. I'd have your pale eyes as my most deserving audience."

Moments in which He unbounded His salacious side were quite hard to come by, so whenever He felt bitten by the lust-bug, i made it my mission to push His lubricious buttons. i didn't have to do much. And i knew it. i knew to do nothing except uplift my cheekbones, squint, and purple my face. He knew how much of me was music. Therefore, anticipating a long orgasmic end wasn't unreasonable at all.

i was aware of His singing capabilities, and The Man i Love was aware of my craze. Even before He shook the rest of our story.

When with a smooth laugh He stretched His lips, exposing His unusually deep dimples, a feeling of dissatisfaction overtook my views.

"Hypothetically," He spouted, killing all of my delusive expectations. Sadly, once again, unjustly dragging me back to my seedy dreams.

Even still, when freed from my madness, i think about the things i could've said to avoid the ensuing moments; to make The Man i Love realize that which had forever been our truth.

i wouldn't have to be so deeply soaked in the marinade of the puzzling life we woefully created. Had i said 'sure!' and just stayed there. Or, had i just been a bit more ruttish. Maybe then, we would've been so much more. Maybe then, unmasked and confident, we'd truly be.

nothing more fatal than
trusting your heart to a timid

The Man i Love carried a leg-stretching figure; was cloaked with savory meat; He wore nifty beauty and was groovily built. The Man i Love was marked by a fullness of flavor. i remember our second gaze. Every so often, i'm still raided by the avid memories. i could never avoid the elevation on my cheeks when reliving moments of just the two of us. Like when, under that dark silky sky, with a vibrant three-sixty spin, i was made to fly. My little black dress reached the stars as The Man i Love arranged me on His shoulders, forming, with my curves, a hug meant to smash bones– He was clocked with savory meat. And, once i knew, my legs were floating shy parallel to His. i reached highs only one of us will ever reach.

Much the same as permanent tattoos, traces of His veins are still drawn along my form. In spite the twists and turns in my heart, i wear them like they're the best pain i ever felt; like these are the most beautiful marks life has ever given me. No shower took our moments down the drain. And time purged absolutely nothing. Even after the April winds, hugs of various kinds – clocked with savory meat and otherwise – His are still nicely residing on my ways. The well-fitted, leg-stretching figure He carried had always been the secret for the best hugs. i've always loved just how His arms slid right through my shoulders when we stood. In truth, surely because of it, mixed with the lines of my burly neck, are still prints of all of His breath-taking grips – every notable impression of His succulent arms. The bumps over my body are still His bold hands tying me like a prey; there was no rush on His part. He made me breathless, dragged my lips up to His and linked our bodies like enticed magnetic screws.

Naturally, He hungered for more. The Man i Love displaced His right hand from my waistline and placed it on my neck touching His left. Our mouthy sauces traveled back-and-forth leaving a powerfully unique taste on my tongue. Fries, orange juice, and iced tea— there and then, dinner was shared. Despite the time grown between us; despite the lives that followed; even despite all of the other kisses i savored, it's Him i feel gummed on my throat. The agitated stream in which i deepened, still washes my mouth away every time i bury my emotions with aching swallows. It's Him I feel!

The Man i Love cracked a wall with my back. He wanted my pain to be His pleasing doing. So it was. With His right hand calmly pulling my box-braids, His left around my neck, He asked my flaming tongue to the dance of her life. Up- and-down they went, mine and His, twisting, as desperate as they were. i will never forget the first day we stirred our juices.

We watched the sun slip into darkness at a pace that deeply ailed. Knots of the corset-belt crushing the butterflies in our stomachs were the markings of our longing. The night had on angry whispers, still we let the winds have our parts. We gave in. He took me by my skirt and made Himself known. A kiss later, still outside the subway station, surrounded by clueless, gut-wrenching, and equally infatuated doubletons—part of His index skimmed my lower boldness. He did shy away from further ventures; but not before letting His second finger from the thumb, travel up a bit and meet the hardened black olives on my chest. Much to my regret, the action was still through my little black dress, but the reaction emulated the most sizzling skin-to-skin contact all over my length and breadth. With the thin, especially chosen piece of clothing venting my curves; comprising me in the most dripping dalliance, The Man i Love set aside a few more venturous seconds for Himself before we had to move on.

The wind bathed the night, and the night wrapped us up in a delightful cold. Other than a few lost plastic bags floating around, the streets were quiet. We were even able to smell the adhesive friction of a train nowhere to be seen. We heard beatings of tired and forlorn hearts very well known to those streets. They went through what felt like another lengthy night, while we struggled to make the seconds last. i was made to fly. And just when i thought heaven had finally reached us, a mockingbird's blasting tune embellished the out-most-sphere.

The moment felt like a passage of a well-written romantic novel; like an ending of a cheerful movie; and like the bridge of a very long-and-profound song. Or maybe i was just too far away from reality to see anything else.

The flaming smell of yet another train going through the rails reminded me just how far i still had to go. Apart from that, its whistle reminded me of the danger of hovering longer.

At a pace to blind and with whispers to chill, i unglued my orange-belte(d)-black-dress from the garms He had on and swore goodbye.

The cold hugged me without hesitation, showering avid windprints all across my body. Outside, to a sky wearing no moon, darkness was everything. And, to me, The Man i Love ceased to be the girdle smashing my butterflies; the image furnishing my eyes; and the clinch mapping out my bones. Ours was the distance!

A few steps away from Him, i couldn't help but wonder about the moment that had just gone to past. About the words neither of us said—and even the ones we did chose to say, however vaguely. The distance between us sent me to an island of whys. Then, with the cold again settled into my pores; with the fire in my belly fueled afresh, i thought about the things i swore to never do, and yet did. i filled my mind with what i knew to be His most prurient urges and allowed myself to smile with no fear.

That twinkle was only the second time we had the pleasure of each other's presence. As quick as it may read, it was then that we truly enjoyed ourselves with the vehemence we hid behind all of those ear-burning phone calls. We locked eyes with sweet reticence, more so me than Him. *Bold* was always an accurate description of The Man i Love. We smiled full of expectations, and hugged like teenagers in a dark movie theater. Right there and then, we allowed ourselves to expose flaming cravings. All that had long been suppressed. We let go of any and all repressing rules, however self-inflicted. For the nights rolling in bed smiling to the ceiling; for all the lunches that were but heart-stirring; for all we foresaw, we had to have found the moment; and that had to be it.

A few miles away from Him, with my far end rested on a worn down sit of an old coach, i thought of nothing else. As the train hissed and screeched making headway, the distance between me and The Man i Love grew longer.

To embrace that particular point in time; to grasp the nettle of the overnight wonders; to appreciate the darkening views; perhaps to see Him again, to feel Him again; to get closer, i leaned my braided head against the glazed window of the train and followed its heartbeat. Only my eyes couldn't keep up with the lights on the subway. It took two or three flashes to close both of them for good. And soon after that, it was night in me too. i saw nothing else!

As i swallowed my own breath, time and again, i began to unriddle all the soppy hand-holdings, the silences, the stares, and even the giggles. A few gobbles after, i gifted myself way more than just the boldness of His forefinger:

The Man i Love did more. His right hand assertively grabbed my right bosom. It wasn't just one of the members caressing my northern valley; no, His entire hand went looking for my womanity. And there, it squeezed silent groans out of me.

Before The Man i Love strove to cover up my silences, preventing the outing of the scream He had just provoked, He took the hand assigned for that task behind my neck. A dainty kiss followed. The Man i Love felt hard!

With my eyes still closed, i saw The Man i Love break a promise. Still, all i heard was: 'I adore touching what's mine;' no other sound registered. i could never confine that man, nor could i ever obstruct justice. My ever-bone-dry figure deserved His completely and altogether!

As the train operator announced the last stop, a tightening feeling rushed to my gullet making an announcement of its own: we had reached the end. The Man i Love understood.

He was driven by His values, cautioned by His morals; inherently kind. He prided Himself in making good decisions, and He had always accounted for His bad ones. i recall the first time we met: we were both volunteering somewhere. We exchanged words, but only the ones we didn't say got stuck. In our reflections were the warm looks that shook us to the core.

"Give me your phone."
"My phone!?" i asked

i knew Him then.

The Man i Love had never been timid. He had always had enough courage for an entire football team. He's confidence had forever been unshaken. And His fears had never been greater than His ambitions. That's the man to whom i assured my heart. The one and only man that numbed my senses entirely.

The Man i Love gently took the phone from my hand, dialed His own number with egotistical confidence, and, after a speedy call, handed it back to me, smirking. "Wasn't so hard, was it?!" His dimples went even further.

"Maybe not!" my lighted eyes were reply.

not all bright moments
turn into great photos

The Man i Love appeared to have had an oversimplified idea of multiple things; important things, for that matter. As we gestured and smiled, He sounded terribly strait-laced, to the extent of inciting concern. In spite of that, i dared to prove myself wrong.

"What a cute accent you have!"

i almost did not believe He uttered those doltish words; it just couldn't have been The Man i Love, so i tried not to take offense. It wasn't my first time hearing such a pointless, yet fair comment. What's more, i'd never kept my *outsider* status a secret; on the contrary, that had always been the seedbed of my pride.

"Yes, Mother is my home!"

"Mother?" His perplexity was sharp.

i definitely loved to bear wittiness to His gaping face. Seeing the lines forming at the ground above His eyes was oddly satisfying. The lanky frowns adorning His expression were signs of His uneasiness. Even His posture changed. At that point, His curiosity served me as fuel. The Man i Love wanted more and, there i was, willing to provide just that—more.

"Mother is what i warmly call the place i left my navel-string. She's my always home."

"i've never heard anybody speak of their birth-place with such love, with such regard. I've definitely seen pride before, but girl, you take it to a different level—" not my words!

The Man i Love locked me up in the flames of His arms; took me by His heaviness. i had never seen Him so brightened. Speaking about our bloodline caused Him to display the most glowing smile i had ever seen. And, right there and then, our bodies wildly commingled.

To be honest, His admiration came out slightly irritating. i was tired of all the goosy comments. Not that The Man i Love made any such notice, but supposing the contrary just seemed callow considering how He started. Every other conversation about roots ended up being nothing but a lecture i was forced to give. Honestly, i didn't want that.

i was still unaware of the extent of His tidings. Up to that point, our conversations had only been about matters of the flesh. It scared me that The Man i Love could have been just like the others. Those that saw me as Colobus' neighbor. Normally i would quickly retract myself from such vexing engagement. i would choose to save my patience. But i'm glad i gave myself a chance to further engage.

"I've dreamed about walking barefooted along the coastline of Saint Anthony. I swear! There is frankly nothing more breathtaking."

My eyes widened, vast enough to set a city ablaze. My bare skin sharpened, a forest of bare thorns bristling to life. I stared at the man I loved as if our gaze were meeting for the first time, charged with the electric thrill of discovery.

"I think that's one of the most precious places there is," He went on to profess.

It took a while until i decoded His aspiration. For the time being, with my eyes still aligned with His, i let myself undust the long unused geography maps held in the deep ends of my memory. That was pretty helpful.

"I only hope She doesn't get destroyed as well," His soliloquy sounded like a prayer.

"Oh, you mean Santo Antão!—"I had to make Him pronounce it the way natives do.—"You people and your bad habit of changing everybody and everything," i added. "The proper way to pronounce it is: sätu a täw. Please, don't colonize us again." i laughed, but He knew i was responding with forethought.

"Wait a minute, why are you getting mad at me? You know me better than this."

i figured The Man i Love was right.

I realized The Man i Love was right. Few knew of places like these, especially those Nana called *mundele*, the pale-faced ones—a term that, of course, didn't apply to Him. For Him to hold such deep knowledge of this hidden, misunderstood world was more than impressive; it was magnetic. He awakened the restless seeker of wisdom within me, stirring an insatiable thirst to savor life through the brilliance of His mind. Every truth felt like a secret shared just between us, sacred and rare, and I felt myself drawn deeper, craving not only His thoughts but the soul that held them.

Our conversation followed its own course. He must've shared a lot, but i had my ears almost completely shut. My sight had to stand unfailing as i committed myself to finding every single detail of the tempting frame that sheltered His mind.

His buccal movements were something other than what He intended them to be. i don't think i ever took the necessary time to truly notice His eyes: dark at first sight, then much lighter when exposed to day-light. It had so much life, it plagiarized an almost- gone sunset. The way they matched the two precious mounts bellow His eyes, was the most blinding thing i had ever seen. His genuinely was the only real angelic face i had ever encountered.

i may have missed the opportunity to lightly, dearly and, frankly go through every inch of His surface, but i did.

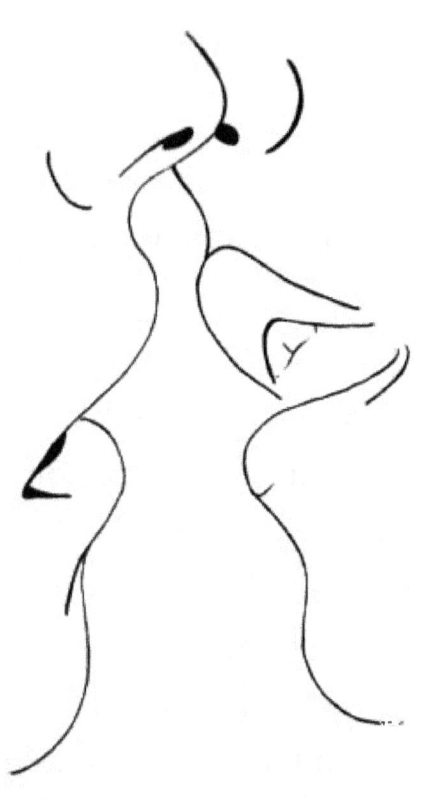

The Man i Love wore the most cunning face. It bore a downiness like no other. i especially appreciated His dimples. Those discrete dimples. Nothing else caused His smile to gleam whiter than the highest clouds; to shine brighter than the biggest stars, or; to feel truer than life. Aww! Those dimples. The Man i Love had always known just how much i wanted to enjoy myself making His grace bloom. And i did.

His athletic trunk rested comfortably on top of mine. There was some concern affixed to my gaze, but i was totally willing to be torn apart. i wanted to be taken places i'd never even dare to dream. No control needed. Along with the noise the bed was making, probably because of its old age, my songs filled up the night. i chanted His name in a note high enough to render anyone deaf. More came out with it. i allowed myself to love that pain. i did the one thing only i could.

The spreading of my lips. The shrill sound of my mouth. The bashful movements of my legs. The aggressiveness of my hands. They were all in favor of our pleasure. i wasn't willing to let any unfair moral restrain the lusty-woman begging to come out. He wanted me. The Man i Love wanted His out-of-this-world moment. i saw Him tying our hands together, causing our fingers to intertwine. i felt His callused-hand elevate the back of my center. The touch was overwhelming! i saw both of His eyes stare at me like i was bread amidst famine. I saw more. With all of that carnal-fury, He showed wanting nothing but a breath-taking moment worth remembering. The Man i Love wanted me. And i wanted me even more. i wanted to know who i could be. i wanted to meet the one long-hidden in me.

The Man i Love had always known just how much i wanted to enjoy myself making His happiness bloom. So i did.

Regardless of how loud life would get, we would find comfort in having each other's company again and again. Under the frenzied sky of an open day, or under the calming night, we knew who we came to be.

In the conversations i had with The Man i Love, He always proposed being the most reserved. Of course He rushed into denial every time i confronted His arguments. i would negate even then. However, whenever i was left with my own madness, i would wonder: maybe He knew something i didn't. The man i had on my loony moments did not match that of the lucid ones, i just insisted on believing. Maybe He knew something then.

i have always lived for my lunacies. The Man i Love had me in heaven. i felt my blood travel up to my throat and out of my mouth with each sucking. He'd absorb my juices just as easily as a baby did his mother's milk:

ripping clothes, braking heals, losing earrings, smearing skin—completely giving up control. With a dark mind and stormy body, The Man i Love overstrained me entirely. He fitted perfectly in my head. In its mess, He was always more than what He showed. He was never intentionally hiding anything; it was just life. i know it all too well: once a heart has been wronged, it takes a lifetime to trust again. But, i didn't fear the strength of His frustrations because i knew how to awaken His faith. i knew The Man i Love. i knew him very well!

i knew His dimples deepened whenever He was exceedingly happy. i knew the frowns on His face lasted as long as His rage. i knew why He kissed with His eyes partially opened. i knew how much He loved playing football. That was His life! The Man i Love liked being seen; being cared for; feeling heard. i knew it as much as i knew He wouldn't like to notice my distraction. i had to go back.

"It's an old dream of mine to leave footprints on the vastness of the Sahara Desert," The Man i Love issued a deep sigh.

"That's beautiful!" so did i.

Our conversation stayed on course, warm and open. The Man i Love spoke of His most shattered dreams, shared bittersweet memories of his father, and let Himself imagine a future yet to come. With each word, He unfolded parts of Himself I hadn't yet seen, like secrets surfacing from deep waters.

"You should really think about joining me. For sure we'd have a lot of fun—" And there they were: the deep dimples.

i wanted to show Him all Mother had to offer. Tell Him of all Her fifty-plus daughters. Make sure He knew of their grounds. i wanted to pray with Him at the highest mountains; wet our bodies in the most beautiful waterfalls.

"Maybe I should."

i knew i sounded vague.

i learned from an early age that a smile could be just as impactful as any other sharp weapon. So, i let one follow my answer. The Man i Love understood that my hesitation to rush into His dreams had nothing to do with what i felt. Mine was love never to be questioned, but i couldn't just take that leap blindly. Ours could never be treated like a mere infatuation. Our most cherished desires were not to be lost in empty promises. The foundation of our lives had to be steady.

"Maybe? Don't wanna show your land?"

With my palm placed on His chin, i brought His face closer to mine; stared right into His sunset-like eyes; and freed another smile, only brighter. Just as The Man i Love started to believe that was everything, i declared: "Believe me, i want nothing more."

it's okay that i love you
but i must love me more

Our shoes were supposed to get stuck between the beautiful Black Rocks at Pungo Andongo. We were both supposed to dust our feet on Kilimanjaro's grounds. Lose our clothes somewhere among the highest trees in the Congo Basin. Shower with the most sizzling sunbeams the Sahara has to offer. We should have allowed all those stubborn winds in Lake Turkana to bathe us with their piercing chills. Dallol would be our warmth. We would spend our days eating the spiciest foods in the streets of Onitsha. And, at night, our life would be poetry. With any luck, we'd be happy. We had it all planned. Perhaps i did. i was ready to introduce Him to Mother. i trusted She would love Him as much as i do.

The Man i Love wanted to leave His prints on the most precious places there were. That was the first of His biggest dreams. He told me so. Thence my readiness, which, of course, was nothing surprising, for i was always poised for Him. Mine was love never to be questioned. i wanted nothing more than to show Him my land. All of its parts.

My hair. This beautiful-luminous-and-strong strands, like the branches of an imbondeiro tree, each one alive with the green pulse of nature. i wanted Him to see. The Man i Love deserved this glimpse of His dream: His fingers threading through my roots, His nose drawn to the earthy scent they exhaled. i could picture His smile, captivated by their fullness, their quiet majesty. This is what i wanted to share with Him: a crown ruling by inspiring. My hair, reaching toward Him like roots seeking water. Each strand holding stories of generations woven with resilience, my hair.

My Face. This beautiful-vast-surface that is as smooth as the sweetest black plum out there. In its entirety, flawless. i wanted Him to see. The Man i Love deserved to wake up next to it, every day for the rest of His life. It would be the first thing He saw every morning and, the very last thing before night became true. That was the dream. i wanted Him to see my well-spread nose with large ways to know nothing but His scent. He'd realize that only one matched His, my face.

My neck. This long-and-juicy adorn mimicking that of Mother's tallest giraffes. Being the sexiest of them all. That's what i wanted Him to see. The pillar of my elegance. i wanted Him to plant kisses all over its ways. To swallow the strength of my flavor. The Man i Love would have to tilt my neck a bit, suck every last of my scrawniness, and make my skin purple. That's exactly what i wanted. The Man i Love staining the lines on my neck.

Our race would even match the grains of Lovina, plagiarizing its darkness. Like never before, time would have been what it actually is, an illusion. The Man i Love would get lost in the emptiness around my screams. He would fear to lose me, but i would assure Him that pain was life itself. Then, stiffened to my trunk He would keep on going through the course of His dream.

My chest. These firm, skyward breasts, hardened by His freezing touch. The Man i Love would've learned just how filling they can be. i wanted Him to see, to gaze as i revealed my weakness, tracing with the palm of my hand the places where i hid my most electric chills. i wanted Him to feel. To touch both, as i raked my nails along the length of His back. That's what i wanted. My polished nails anchored to His skin, pulling Him closer. The Man i Love was meant to rest here, to find refuge in the rise and fall of my chest.

My legs. These lengthened-radiant sticks. These two pretty and mighty engines. The cranes that take my beauty all around. They would intertwine with His. That's what i wanted Him to see. Their knot. i wanted Him to take them by His hand and give 'em to the skies. While He planted kisses along their longness, spreading them chills, He was supposed to finally show His manhood. i wanted Him as a whole-man. That was the dream. The Man i Love lost between my legs.

My Mother's daughter, at last, His. i wanted Him drunk with her warmness. His hunger satisfied. That's what i wanted. The Man i Love was supposed to take up all of my juices while i did His. That was the dream. Mine and His. Both of ours. The Man i Love wanted nothing more than be shown to my land. He told me so. And, for that, i was there too. Completely naked. Because mine was love never to be questioned.

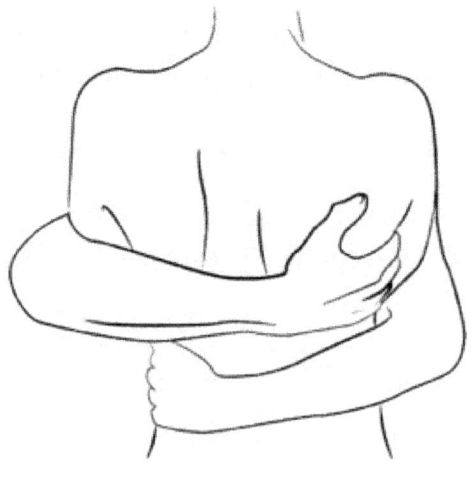

Our bodies were fused, our souls bound, forever entwined—or so we thought. Perhaps only i did. Our warmth blended into a single, seamless heat, radiating the intoxicating power of a bond deeper than infatuation. This wasn't something to question, to betray, or to resist. It was the destiny of our spirits, an unspoken vow neither of us should have dared to break. It was life and death intertwined; a force as inevitable as breath.

As we surrendered ourselves, it became clear that our desire was one forever kept. We got lost in the upshots of that truth. Our most cherished desires were secured in the most trusting promises. The foundation of our lives stood straight. Never a conversation about roots had an ending so grand. It was clear at that fundraising event. It was even more so when my randy eyes encountered His juicy figure for the second time. When He held me tight i knew then too. He was The Man i Love.

i saw Him.

Even when He was dawn.

i awaited Him.

Even when He was gone.

i felt Him.

Even when He was cold.

i reached Him.

Even when He was unsure. i wanted Him.

Even when He was impure. i held Him.

Even when He was aloof.

i kept Him.

Even when He was theirs.

i kissed Him.

Even when He was dry.

i trusted Him.

Even when He was proof.

i loved Him.

Even when He was lie.

i don't know when my body was taken from His. When the fastenings of our souls came undone. To this day, my mind can't decipher how she came to no longer revere Him. At some point, The Man i Love wasn't the one behind my audio-phonic interactions. And that was just fine. My ears didn't mind the cold, neither wailed my body for finally resting sound on the bed where, now, i alone dreamed. In case of low temperature, i was ready to just pull up the covers that laid still by the footboard of my bed. i suddenly could enhance my own sanity.

Whether we spoke or not, my days were all right. Not painfully long, nor disturbingly short. That's How I was. i got used to His delays in keeping His promises. Maybe i no longer cared. The un-replied messages ceased to bother. i stopped worrying about Him checking His phone to return calls because mine, finally, wasn't replete with outgoings.

At that point, The Man i Love wasn't connecting His voice to the pinnacle of my foregone-sanity. That ceased to happen! Our unclothed talks made their way to the quietude of the past and decided to stay.

"What are you wearing?" He would ask.

There would be deep dimples; for sure. But it would be silent. The Man i Love would whisper His desires in the acuteness of my ear.

"I wish I was over there."

"So do i!" i would already be wet.

i would feel the breeze make its way into my insides, accompanied by His leering voice. i would be sent off to uncontrollable cravings. "i'm wearing absolutely nothing," i'd reply. "It's only me, my skin, and i, stretched in here—" aah! The Man i Love would die.

My sleeping positions stopped being a part of our conversations. So did His.

That no longer was who we were.

Back when, The Man i Love would push all my boundaries aside. We would watch our bodies get lost in the mix of our madness. i remember a time my phone almost became Him: It was dark outside, but the lights of our closed eyes were such that no stain was left unseen. i remember all His heaviness on top of me. "GOD!" That wasn't just me thinking. "Good thing there's no tomorrow, or else i'd miss it." i thought to myself as i felt my posterior being thrown against the wall and onto the bed. Those were the doings of His hefty hands. As i heard Him say just how much He wanted to be there—deep down—i looked at my phone like it was actually one of those godly hands of His.

As it turned out, that was no longer who we were. The Man i Love caused our longings to be obsolete. He made Himself unfit.

| *the fastest way to kill a heart* |
| *is leaving it with no answers* |

My blood ran pale, washed out. i had never stood in that place before, yet i found an unsettling comfort in the clear, distilled spirit from the eastern lands, stolen by one of Mother's most notorious intruders. The numbness of intoxication offered a truce—a dark, quiet peace as the liquor wound through my veins, dulling the edges of my pain. My legs stretched long and moved in a twisted, winding path, a directionless journey of their own making. i knew this vertigo wasn't born of the almond-toe pumps i wore that day. It wasn't the darkness wrapped around my feet that disoriented me. It wasn't even the liquor's pull. My heart lay shattered within me, that was all.

And yet, as I hovered on the brink of oblivion, i allowed His image to fill me one last time, chilling and raw, a final haunting of the love i had lost.

The Man i Love wandered around my head. The weight pressing me down was something i had never experienced. All of a sudden, my box-braids were too heavy to let fly. Before, not even when wet, they felt as hefty as His hands. That never happened! i had the fierce blazing of The Man i Love. He made me feel His presence with a blend of the most wicked desires. It was as if He had been let into the most inconvenient moral-conflict of His life, and needed to be rescued by me; by my defiant self. The Man i Love knew i was just the woman for that. My willingness to give up control was something we could have used for our own good. He knew i had never feared the strength of His frustrations. Moreover, He new very well of my ways of shaking His originally malformed faith. i knew The Man i Love. And

He knew that was true, hence His unforeseen presence on my now-placid faculty of reason. i loved nothing but being touched, and well touched. So, in or out of my head, He was welcomed indeed. He wanted a breath-taking moment worth an everlasting remembering. We were about to have that, and much more.

'Why now?' i should have asked myself. i should've at least tried to find out why my eyes were distending again. Why i was, so loudly, forcing out the running drops of my river. Why i was jumpstarting my slim-state. The number of bottles i opened could only have made my figure sick. i should have thought about that. It wasn't good the first time around, so the chances of it getting better were almost nil. It had been a while since we last spoke. The smart thing to do would've been to at least try to know why that was the moment. But i didn't. Instead, i allowed The Man i Love to overtake me once more. To wander around my head and to lose His on my entryways.

i felt the softness of His fro up my left thigh. My knee was high. 'I adore touching what's mine,' The Man i Love made Himself known, plowing my land. Those weren't just words. The spreading of my lips. The flooding on my mouth. The trembling of my legs. Even the reason my belly flattened was Him.

The Man i Love took His tongue on a trip across my chest. From the river-forest downtown to my navel, He made me relinquish the rest of my control. The waves i made with my chubbiness was what i felt. Every lick was a wave of chills. When He went from the scar of the umbilical cord to the lower boundaries of my breasts, He made me beg for more. The songs i sung while wrinkling our bed-sheets were the lines of my request. His name was each one of the thunderous groans. i wanted Him all over. 'If you were

mine, i would touch every single inch of you—
' The Man i Love was true.

Before completely stepping out of the mirth, for the longest second of my life, i was all of that joy. The Man i Love was again on my mind and i didn't ask why. i didn't care. i thirsted for the pain of reliving Him.

My blood was bleached. It had lost all of its reddish brilliance. i knew it was because of the liquid depressant i was treating myself with. And while that was pain, The Man i Love, now on my nipples, was comfort.

He bathed my areola with the pleasing orgasms of His mouth. Gave His tongue the most sodden swirls around the darkness of my breasts. The Man i Love knew where and just how to bite. So, He did. Again and Again.

But that was no longer what we were. So, i should've asked the questions i was feeling. Maybe then i would've protected myself from the heartbreak that followed.

The Man i Love blew my mind. He unleashed all my flowers. He made heaven feel like hell, only better.

Before mincing my heart, The Man i Love was sweet. He looked at me, fondled my face, and embed a kiss between my brows sprouting rainbows from my cheeks. Ahh... Nirvana! No better way to rest. The Man i Love had me in His arm. He let the weight of my shoulders be His. And, to stretch the moment; to make it so that each second lasted much longer; to get lost in all we could've done; to appreciate our satisfaction; perhaps to feel again, He grabbed my hair, passing His hand through the back of my neck, and gave me the most breathtaking kiss. Only my mind didn't want to just stop there. It only took ten drunk pressings. Before long, with the phone then glued to my ear, it was the sharpened rays of His voice i was hearing. Except, then, The Man i Love felt anxious.

"Hey!"

i don't have dimples, but the way my eyes squinted betrayed the rush of joy His voice stirred in me. My cheekbones lifted high, my face flushed deep with that familiar, feverish warmth I'd only felt with Him. He was happiness in its rarest form. Nothing else could make my smile stretch so wide, gleam whiter than clouds, brighter than stars, or feel truer than life itself. Nothing. Nothing but His voice. My greeting came out loud yet rough, a blend of excitement and longing. i wanted to sound like home to Him. i wanted Him to feel at ease, to hear the comfort of familiarity. i thought that if my voice carried the same spark it had in our last shared moment, maybe—just maybe—He'd still be The Man i Love. Maybe He'd feel, even for a heartbeat, that time hadn't frayed us, that we were still those same souls, bound by reckless, unreasonable fondness. But beneath my words, my heart pounded, wild and frantic, threatening to leap from my chest.

"Who's this?"

The Man i Love sounded anxious. His words tumbled out, rushing and trembling. i couldn't see His face, but i didn't need to; i knew those dimples on His sculpted cheeks wouldn't be as deep as they were in our good times. i knew that man. Every inch of Him was etched into my mind. But now i found myself unable to read the lines of His expression, to decode those frowns i feared could be hiding anger. Anger i couldn't bear. My body ached for something else, some familiar comfort. I'd seen The Man i Love in his moments of playful desire, felt the strength of his sensitivity, reveled in his spirited laugh. He could be lighthearted, even mischievous, cracking those dry, sobersided jokes. i knew those sides of Him, all of them. But this—this troubled tone, this edge of unease—was something new, something foreign. The Man i Love sounded shaken, and it left me chilled, realizing there was still a part of Him unknown to me.

"Hey!—" that's how i greeted Him.

"Who's this?—" that was His answer.

For a second, i believed that our conversation would end with those hollow words. Not only that, i believed that our entire relationship would be defined by the fear we both failed to explain. For the first time, The Man i Love took my call with an uneasiness that automatically rejected it.

i decided to understand His frustration. In any case, i had hidden my number. The Man i Love had nothing but an overexcited voice to explain the 'unknown' that had suddenly appeared on His phone-screen. It had been a while since we last spoke. And, considering the time apart, i didn't want to take the risk. i didn't want to be or feel rejected. i wanted to keep my heart intact. i didn't want The Man i Love to know i was the one giving up the dolt silence between us.

"Who... is... this?"

As the Man i Love spelled out the last words i hoped to hear, i felt the lanky frowns forming on the north-side of His face. It wasn't hard to suppose the expression of His inquietude. But, i swear, that was not what i intended. Not too long before all of this, i was invaded by His image. The Man i Love had just spread His mouth's orgasms through the extension of my body. That wasn't a treat i would ever dare to forget. A happy-ending was all i wished to secure with that call.

The plan was simple: trailing a few attempts from His part; a few pushy hello(s); but, prior to Him wearying, i would break the silence and seductively reveal who i was. Better yet, The Man i Love would happily infer. Then, i would eagerly declare my reasons for calling. The sound of my voice was supposed to delight The Man i Love. He was supposed to foreknow my desires and understand my flattering insinuations. If all went well, we'd wish for the exact same thing:

The Man i Love would rush His athletics legs into an oldish-wrinkled pair of pants. He'd anticipate reaching the place where the sky kisses the earth; the moon reflects into the sea, and; the stars just lay, appreciating the moment. My dress would be practical. It'd open from behind dispensing ugly pulls. It would begin with His hands sliding from the top of my scrag, reacting to our lips' succulent meeting. i would lose my shyness; and, every inch of the fallacious modesty i've carried through the years. We would lay in front, on the back, even on top of His still-dented car. Screeches would follow. The outspread of my blaring shouts would be the unveiling of my freewheeling self. My happiness would be thrown into the air—shared with all creatures of the night and given to the unhappy.

No call had ever made me feel so powerful, so alive. The Man i Love did that. i slipped into a short black dress, sleek as midnight, matching the dark glint of my heels, feeling a rare sense of completeness. My heart began to pound the moment He picked up, each beat pulsing with anticipation, with a hope that felt almost tangible.

But then, His voice shattered the spell. It was stripped of warmth, laced with tension—a stranger's voice. His nervousness was a cold blade, slicing through my hopes before they even had a chance to rise.

And then, piercing the silence, another voice. High-pitched, sharp, and brimming with hostility:

"Who da hell are you?"

The words hung there, chilling and final, leaving me hollow. At that moment, my world shifted, unraveling in a way i could not stop.

if every deception was death
there would be no remains for remembrance
fortunately, i know to shower with my tears

It was my fault. i should've known to stop. i should've just enjoyed the invigorating memories of His last invasion. i should've embraced the pinnacle of my contentment and halted. i should have realized the grounds of His frightened state. i could at least have spared myself the slaying deception. It was on me not to ignore the signs. The Man i Love did indicate being unavailable. He did. So, it was my fault. The rays of His voice were not as polished as in our past exchanges. In all the time i have known this dauntless man, never a silence was unfilled. Either i'd adorn the ambiance with a close-lipped smile or, The Man i Love would straight-up issue a laugh to awake. That's how we were. i should've seen.

i surely expected some resistance. The person to whom i offered my shameless self wasn't impatient in the slightest. However, i would've been fine with a little display of frustration. i would've fully understood displeased screams—or even, empty threats about abruptly terminating the call. i was ready to salvage the mood with the alluring sound of my voice, which The Man i Love greatly revered. And, i was confident that was still the case. If needed, i would gladly offer The Man i Love a second memorable call. We would get lost in our most scandalous longings. i was ready. Unfortunately, what i wasn't ready for, was whatever He decided to be.

In a shorter time than i care to recall, The Man i Love wanted to leave His prints on the most precious places there were. That was the first of His biggest dreams. He told me so. And i—as fervid as i was—didn't waste any time trying to make it came to pass. Mine was love never to be questioned—that's a truth i've always strived to attest. Therefore, my mind dared to anticipate the unfolding of His aspiration. All of this, before the distilled booze. The Man i Love was all over my Mother's daughter even when that wasn't who we were. Never a conversation about roots had an ending so grand. Ours was matchless. And even before a call completely broke my heart, i allowed His image to invade me. The Man i Love was true once again. That's how much i loved Him—i love Him! So, yes, His cold response left me in pieces.

The Man i Love razed our lives. My blood was already bleached. i was left baffled. Left with no answers. Forced to dig through our chronicle and find a plausible explanation for His distraught demeanor. Anything to aid understanding and preserve sanity, which, with that call, was at an all-time low.

In the wake of crushing sorrow, i felt an urgent need to find a corner to weep. My numb shoulders pressed against the cold, unyielding walls, leaving faint stains as i crawled toward the only solace my body could find in the aftermath of that wretched moment. Disbelief drained every ounce of strength from me. I had to let myself collapse before the weight of it did something worse, something irreparable.

Honestly, i couldn't fully grasp what had happened. Nothing sounded rational enough to keep my sanity from unraveling, no explanation strong enough to stop the decay creeping in. i knew i'd heard His voice, razor-sharp and unmistakable, yet the content of our exchange lingered like a dark hallucination, too surreal to trust.

We had never been this fractured. Never. The Man i Love and i had always drifted through endless conversations that would leave our faces lit with quiet smiles—not dried trails of salt tracing the path of silent tears. No, that was never us. Despite life's harshest ambiguities, love had always bound our moments. But now, that bond felt fragile, like something thin and frayed, slipping through my fingers and leaving me cold.

Cross footed—with my head where His once was—i dared to relive recent events. i hoped to decipher my pain: Perhaps i've just heard His sister's voice. Perhaps i did because He had one such relative. He told me so. On many occasions, for that matter. Maybe that was, in fact, one of His fewest truths. Those were the dire thoughts in my mind's disarray.

i wasn't sure of what had just happened. i knew nothing of the woman that so unfairly and insolently spoke to me. i knew nothing of her anger. i barely understood His. The Man i Love baffled me, and there was nothing i could tell her for i too struggled to understand His reasoning. His jitters were quick to undercut all my hopes. Her unflattering voice gored a sword into my heart, and i felt as though i couldn't pull it out. She could not be the embodied kindness He'd so fondly describe in our conversations. No way she was that fine being. Those were the comforting thoughts i desperately harvested. Regardless of the pain, i refused to grant Him my demise. The Man i Love would not be the end of me. That could never be so.

One thing i knew for sure: i heard a female voice. Not as melodic as mine, but one nonetheless. As i found myself deprived of proof, i decided to believe that was His sister merely being protective of the one we both loved. The Man i Love was the youngest of three. And, as per one of His confessions, closest to His sister. So, it made sense.

Regardless of the call's ramifications, which could've very well been avoided, i decided to shower with my own tears and allow ourselves a future. Unfortunately, when a call from The Man i Love didn't hasten my morning, i knew it couldn't be so simple.

the foolishness of love
is not to be understood
such pain is not endured
spreading kisses away

The colored sky conceived a blazing sun. One beyond compare. Its beams roasted the skins of the brightest leaves as they danced to the most forceful winds. The redolent flowers spread ever spurring flavors through the air. Heaven had never shown herself so wide, so lucent. Never! Never had i felt such light penetrating my pores. It was indeed a day to remember. It was a Sunday still clouded by the events of a grueling Friday, yes, but it was a new day at last. Regardless of it all, i felt so depleted that not even my lies made me any less sad. i lost weight without running; my belly lost what in fact was never there—i was no more. And, yet, the scariest thing, at that moment, was realizing my unconcern.

"Hey, girl! How you doing?"

"Heyyy! I'm all right. How 'bout you?!"

The words flew from my mouth quickly, wrapped in a wide, luminous smile. In truth, i wasn't eager to see my phone light up, especially not with another's name filling the screen. i could, in all honesty, recognize the comfort of a casual call in such a fragile moment. And i did. But deep down, i knew i wasn't ready. My heart wasn't about to listen to my mind's convenient urges. My lips parted, tasting the air with a hint of longing, my eyes slipped halfway shut, and a shiver raced through me—all signs of the surprise stirring within, the unexpected ache that came unbidden. In that instant, i realized that no call could reach the part of me still anchored to Him.

"Wanted to check on you, hear your voice and stuff—" he avowed with happiness.

The talk went on with some breathing on his part, and almost nothing on mine, as I was gravely stunned. It was T, and i wasn't expecting him. Not for nothing, but T was oblivion. His name wasn't even among the ones i'd seek to remember after the harrowing feelings were gone. No matter how short it was. T was a past i had decided to leave there.

He was undeniably good—a good man he was. But not wholly to my taste, i'm afraid. He wasn't tall enough—not as tall as The Man i Love. Not quite how i favored. He wasn't high in stature, cloaked with savory meat, very-well built; that was not him. And, for my ill-luck, i knew precisely. T was a little pale, though exquisite in his own way. Often trying to be funny. Not too different from The Man i Love. T was desirable, i don't refute that. He was worthy of my attention, sure; however, The Man i Love was far more—perfect in His imperfections; just the right ingredient for my joy. And, in spite of my efforts to change the recipe, no one proved themselves more ideal.

T, this delightful yet unexpected caller, didn't learn much about my affection during our short-lived connection. i don't deny that it was pleasing, but a conclusion was bound. He didn't understand that affection was not to be begged. Mine in particular. To have my affection was to have robbed it with lethal passion. That was my most unsettling thirst. And, perhaps by misfortune—apart from his decent looks—T lacked what was needed to keep me. i was never a woman to entertain virile insecurities. The Man i Love was well aware of it. So, i presume that was the reason for my frigid and quick conversation with T.

In light of the awkward pleasantries, i allowed my figure to revert. i had on a velvet blouse that matched my sadness exactly. The boots that embellished my far-extended legs were colored just like the poncho derailing the cold. There was also a twill turtleneck—a collar-fitting apparel warming my ears. When my phone could finally find its way back to the solid-black purse matching my linen pants, i drew a deep sigh and returned to the tears that had flooded my morning. The doing in itself felt like a much needed relief.

As soon as exhaustion dried my tears, i realized where i was. When the first bus stopped, i knew i had to collect myself and endure another. And, so i did. However, on that occasion, i manipulated the mood to my advantage. The ride was to last a little over thirty minutes, long enough for an additional dose of my daily deaths, my quiet screams of agony. Seeing that i had no choice but share the space with those unnamed souls—some more miserable than i—i dared to admire the scenery, to pleasure myself with diverging memories. Following the sudden call, i settled for seeing T as a nice change, as a temporary remedy for aches incited by The Man i Love.

The atmosphere was still ravishing after all. While i was foolishly blinding myself, some were dancing, others were playing; there were even those who opted for the darkness of a kiss. They moved their heads like they believed in nothing else. As a matter of fact, witnessing the young couple with matching sneakers was rather enjoyable. They reminded me of dear T—of his misplaced romanticism. It was a passion with no place in such rough world. i waited for him to realize; then i left.

Although i was a bit surprised, T's call brought in an almost forgotten happiness. That's what i called to mind. His charming touch. His soft hands on my back. Even when his acts were scandalous he insisted on showing that he wasn't a mere savage. Even deep in my roots T was delicate. i saw it. i felt it enough times. It was as if nothing was more important. The Man i Love was nothing like T. But perhaps, He was just what i needed.

A dark-themed palette across the torso made the jalopy seem appealing. i only regretted that the seats didn't have the same sensation. The fumes eluding like isolated farts from the tail end anticipated my arrival.

Each tree along the way became grief. The songs in the woodland were no longer effective lullabies. It was as if the talented birds had lost their muse. From afar, the sun remained a strong flame burning brightly. But she was all alone. i felt her. The sound of children playing easily turned into the most hateful melody. The view of the scenery supposed to remedy my aches failed to satisfy.

i was boiling inside. My face overdressed itself with frowns of desperation. It was as if i had forgotten to pretend strength. Like i could embarrass myself at any moment, screaming with the honesty of a peeved child. Only, as luck would have it, time started appreciating my hard-attained self-control.

Just when i considered handing over yet another victory to The Man i Love, the rusty doors of the bus faced me unshut. The walk would usually last about fifteen minutes. i decided i didn't have more than half that time to reach home. i ran. Immediately after i unlocked the gates, i rushed inside and found a corner to tattoo my aroused misery. To take an additional dose of my daily deaths. And, to finally unquiet my screams. To freely be.

With my desire redeemed, i planted on the floor, the two cushions supporting my rear beauty. The appetizing tushes i proudly carry. The two most accurate representation of Mother. i let each one of my lovely and chubby cheeks harden on the freezing tiles of the living room. What's more, i slid my back against the pimples on the wall strewing my tears around. The hellish state of my being exposed my eyes to an alarming degree. It became clear that i had forced out all my sadness. Withal, by my good fortune, soon i wept no more.

i took my palms to a trip up north. They skimmed the prominence of both my cheeks with affection. The lines on the inner surface of my hand received the last of my distress. Tears run through them like waters in a frantic lake. In the end, their subtle return was marked by a drought. The grin that flew along with my arms was not a prayer. Not quite! It was instead the sign of an urgent request. Or, better yet, a demand never to be rejected.

i willed those self-serving, so-called immortal beings to leave me in peace. i didn't scream—my strength, the force of my body, had long since abandoned me. i didn't scream. But they heard me. Those so-called gods felt the fury of my silent pleas. They had to. They insisted on tearing The Man i Love away from me, and with that, i vowed to stop caring for their hollow promises. i turned my back on them, seeking them no more. Instead, i buried every ounce of faith i had left in the quiet darkness, where even they could not reach.

T was a good man. His joy was woven into my well-being. He wanted to care for me like the earth cradles the last drops of late-spring rain—with a desperate devotion, nurturing life as if every drop were a final gift, coaxing fruit from an ever-thirsty soil. He waited for me to surrender, even long after i was gone. T was undeniably good—a man of unwavering kindness and steady intentions. But The Man i Love was different, a persistent, exquisite ache that seeped into my bones. And strangely, that was exactly what i yearned for.

Feigning sleep, my lashes brushed upward, skimming the coolness of my cheeks. No blush marked them, yet my face felt exposed, vulnerable under the weight of memory. Though the ceiling filled my view, shutting my eyes drew me into His presence—The Man i Love. But this time, the dream twisted into something dark, a nightmare so visceral it left me breathless, reaching for anything to hold onto.

The Man i Love had done more than turn away from the sound of my voice; He had forsaken the deepest parts of me, discarded the essence of my soul with a chilling indifference. In that moment, i felt a vast emptiness, a hollow ache where once there was warmth, as if i'd become nothing more than a shadow reaching out for a light that had already faded.

He broke me. His silence broke me. His impatience broke me. His shouts broke me. Even the lanky frowns that once filled His presence had vanished completely, replaced by an unsettling vacancy. It wasn't hard to imagine the expression of His unease—another thing that shattered me. The Man i Love had drawn out every last piece of me. And yet, soon after, my tears dried. With the closing of my eyes, no more fell. For the first time in all my madness, He was only half. The Man i Love was no longer something more; He was merely human. He was still of a tall and wide figure.

Reserved, careful, and quiet, He was the one i'd carried in my deepest desires. He resisted clichés but showed His love in small, tender gestures. The Man i Love would cradle my face, kiss my brow, and bring color to my cheeks. Tender—that was Him. In our private escapes to the future, He'd promise never to be the kind of father who walked away.

Driven by values and grounded by morals, He was inherently kind. Yet, He could press me against a wall, knowing i wanted to yield, to let my pleasure become His. In some dark way, He relished my surrender.

He was unpredictable—nothing like T. Being with Him meant embracing the unknown. For the first time, i saw Him clearly, human in all His flaws and beauty.

Then came the questions, heavy as stones. One echoed louder than the rest: *Why?* Unsatisfied, i redialed His number, craving an explanation—or maybe, just craving Him.

the issue is not loving too much
but losing oneself along the way

My ear felt nothing of the winter chill, and my body offered no resistance; it trusted the decision i'd made. It was, indeed, a day to remember. Though the weight of Friday's wounds still lingered, Sunday felt like a new beginning. i felt anointed by the moon, blessed by the sun, and deeply strengthened by a fierce need to understand. Despite its ugliness, its raw edges, was resolute. The Man i Love would have no choice but to confront me, to explain His nervous evasions, His cold responses, and, most crucially, His chilling disregard for the essence of my soul. i had to confront the parts of Him that had s turned haunting. To hear His version of the truth, I called Him twice more.

"This call has been forwarded to the voicemail of..." i didn't think that it would be easy. On a similar note, i never much cared for that voice. So inconsiderate. So prompt to dismiss. To let down. Hence my hanging up of the phone before i got even more annoyed.

The youngsters were in their little pressed suits. The mothers of their mothers graced their wise braids with massive hats. Everybody else had on their dominical outfits patterned with striking colors. The aura was gelid but pleasant. The wind smelt fresh. A sky stripped of its clouds was the ultimate sign of a new day. A hallowed one. A Sunday.

The embers inflaming my heart—those which were once bliss—in a trice, had the air of a rim posed around my gorgeous burly neck. After the highly annoying pre-recorded message overheated my earrings, i couldn't help but expose my exhaustion. Fall around the place like shred—not hungry, not asleep—somewhat disgusted, and deeply demoralized. Feeling overwhelmed with callow weakness.

To think i gave up is absurd in the least.

As established by the earthly-sphere, with a spin, another sunshine was killed. High notes of golden-pheasants brought me back from the mourning period. Morsels of the birds' music woke me up and spread hard chills through the extension of my body. Besides, on the full scope of my skin, was still the bedspread that hid my nakedness from the night. A new forenoon showed itself upon me.

i caught the sharp dialing tones through the earpiece i wore, each sound a step closer to The Man i Love. His number glowed on the screen in my left palm. i was calm, without fear, yet a strange discomfort coursed through me, an unease that wrapped itself around my resolve.

"This call has been forwarded to the voicemail of..." there it was again, nettlesome.

i knew you wouldn't pick up—an ill sigh.

That was the start of my resolute speech. A storm raged across my face; the thick drops weren't tears, but they stung just the same. They surged forward the moment i yielded to that condescending voice, each drop carrying the weight of words i'd held back for too long.

"just wanted to, uhm.. i wanted to... guess i wanted to know!" - my expression altered.

i couldn't even make up the words to explain those lines to myself. i just couldn't. No matter how short they were. Every bit of my efforts to verbalized them was met with an influx of butterflies into my stomach.

"i just wanted to understand," i added.

My vital unifying force wavered, teetering closer to collapse. i feared i might break before summer. Each heartbeat pulsed like a warning, a fragile reminder of the strength slipping away. Still, i pressed on.

"i was hopping you would tell me what you wanted—what you wished to discuss."

If i told people The Man i Love had called me just a few days before; they probably wouldn't believe. But He did. And, in so doing, most certainly without knowing, He equipped me with the means to escape the embarrassing situation in which i put myself.

"i may have an idea of what it might be, but, as you well know, i much prefer your voice. So, i'll let you tell me. Maybe sing?!"

The Man i Love had seen me verbose, puzzled, flushed—He understood my flirting.

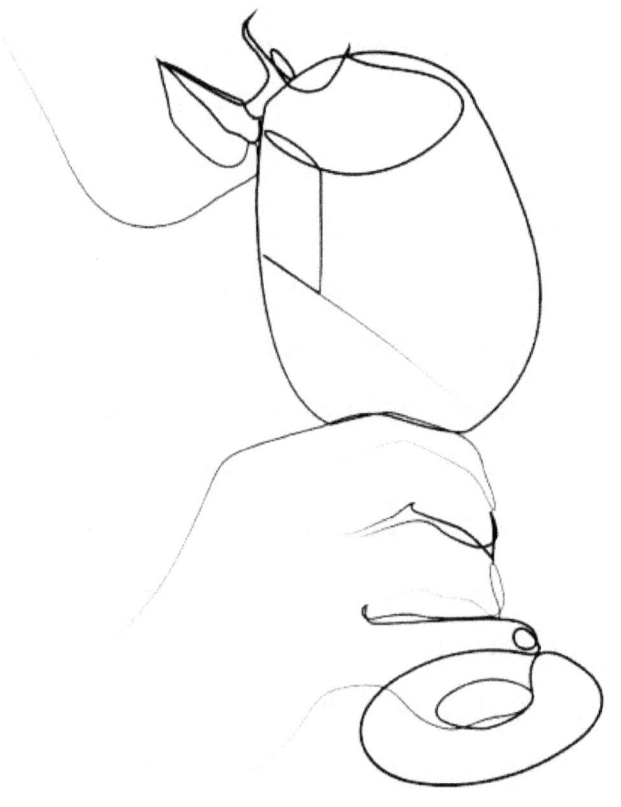

i wondered if He bore me in His mind. Each and every one of my sips was that: a mystified thought. As i allowed nips of the wine to flood my belly, i filled my head with answers i wanted The Man i Love to disprove.

If you see the call i didn't pick up as our final exchange, that's all right—just read my goodbye: i wish you good fortune. i invoke upon you the most advantageous contracts. May you play as superbly as you've always played. Especially with little 'mates of your own. i hope you get to walk barefooted along the coastline of Santo Antão. i really wish that you find the opportunity to bury your prints deep within Mother. i know you'll love Her!

i longed for so much more. The Man i Love deserved more—i knew that! Yet, i saw no sense in pouring myself into a drunken declaration that would fall into empty space, destined to reach no one.

An ashen looking star giving way to another so much more flaming. The pores through one's frame being liberated at last from the closures of the cold night, time and time again. The birdy consort extending their melodic roster each and every morning, making lyrical sounds with the sorrows of lost pedestrians. Even the minutes running to fulfill the hours. All were signs of the passing of the days. Days i survived without Him. Without The Man i Love. Alas, days not engaged in long and dulcet dialogues with Him: the man i so deeply love. Days too hard to endure. Especially that one: the day i missed the most desired and expected call. The one from Him. From The Man i Love.

i'll go. But, know this: i wish you well.

My eyes shamefully surrendered to the powers of that fine fermented juice. i looked at the phone in my hands, shaking—at risk of being dropped—the message i had written was still waiting to be sent. i think i barely realized that. i couldn't have. Not until the morning came. Not until i had slept through that excruciating hangover.

As i finished writing that last line, i fell asleep. In any event, there was no point in losing myself in a drunken declaration of love doomed to reach no one.

We had spent a lot of time talking, and that truth was consuming me more than the devastating pain of, possibly, having lost Him. Luckily, my mind always knew the best ways to take care of me. She took me back to a beautiful moment of ours. i dreamed about the day we planned a perfect date.

The conversation had already taken a rattling provocative turn. Earlier on, we discussed things we would've done to each other had life been fair. Before the ensuing moments, both The Man i Love and i became familiar with the most itching desires we carried for each other.

i laid my aroused self on the back. My bare, hairless body, rested on top of my comfortable Cosy House Luxury sheets. Yes, they were just as marvelous as their fancy name. Full of delight! The Man i Love lowered His voice. He spoke like there was a baby between us, and it couldn't be woke. A logic in which i almost believed; were it not for the fact that His words came out with every intention of awakening my screams.

In that perceptual experience, The Man i Love took care of me like no Rabbit ever did. Our mad bodies became involved in a shivery concern about the subsequent measures they should've taken. They wore no shame, they saw no hurdle, they anticipated no end. Truth be told, all they acknowledged were their desires. His: to awaken my screams. Mine: to allow that, and more. The Man i Love and i went on the most orgastic jaunt of our lives.

Unfortunately, i came around to reality.

i was still under the influence of wine. i had my eyes opened. i just didn't know if i would be able to stand on my feet. They were trembling. My head was spinning too fast. My stomach was wringing. Seated on the age of my bed, as i faced the wall overlooking my breasts—au naturel—i saw my predicament: Hangover, migraines, and stinging butterflies.

All things considered, it was Monday. I couldn't afford to waste another day sobbing, drowning in lament. So, I pulled myself to the shower—quick, cold, and necessary. My aching body, still steeped in hurt, I dressed in the sexiest yet most polished dress in my closet. Then I drove myself to work, each mile a step further from the sorrow I left behind.

look not for love
when dismay is undesired

Green was the color of my shoes. A bit darker, like a young Aspen tree. The D'Orsay pumps were only three inches high. i feared walking was something i had to learn all over again. So, it seemed appropriate: new-beginnings represented on my feet. Despite my adamant efforts to move on, i was weak amidst the urge to over-line my curves with grief, ergo the black dress—as dark as night. On the flip-side, i insisted on moving on. So, with that in mind, i picked out the bodycon dress elongated with floral lace. The lace was green too, matching the pumps perfectly. i was flawless! Mr. John, the security guard, thought exactly the same. He said as much with a wink of his eye. i threw a smile.

"Hey e...!"

"Hello."

"Whoa, why the tone?"

"The tone? Seriously?"

"Never mind. How are things?"

"Fine."

"Is it just me or you're being a bit too curt right now? I know you are not usually like this. So, lemme ask: is everything okay?"

"Like i said: everything is perfectly fine."

"That is just wonderful! I am incredibly happy to hear that. I have been thinking about you. So... I thought I would call."

"What have you been thinking about?"

"You?"

"Okay, but, what about me?"

"Clarissa, what's going on?"

"I'm merely asking for details. Am I also being curt... by asking you that question?"

"No, but..."

"Well?"

"Okay! If you must know, I have been thinking about the fact—the sad fact, i should add—that we haven't really talked in a while and... that... we most definitely should. And... I've also been thinking about how much I've missed you. And, that I should've just called."

"Hmm."

"What? Did I say something wrong?"

"No. Just the opposite, actually."

"What? Heh."

"Is it funny?"

"I didn't laugh."

"That smug tone implied as much."

"Clarissa, you reading too much into it. Could you, please, just tell me what's wrong?"

"Listen, tell me this: did what i say sound odd to you?"

"A bit, yes."

"Why?

"Just to clarify, what... would be... the opposite of wrong... in this case?"

"i think you said just the right things."

"What?"

"That's why i asked if it was funny?"

"Oh, okay."

"Yah!"

"And that's bad because...?

"i never said it was. Now, who's reading too much into things?"

"So?"

"So what?"

"So, why the reaction?"

"Surprise, maybe."

"Mm!"

"What, don't believe me?"

"You've never given me reason to doubt you... It's just that... uhm... hearing that... from you, of all people... feels bittersweet."

"Hmm. And... why is that?"

"Umm... I don't know. It's just that... Look, I know I've always been too weird with using my words—"

"Weird?"

"Shh, Clarissa, please, don't interrupt."

"Sorry, Jerry Rice—"

"Hah, I see you're still funny."

"i didn't give you that nickname... And, although your brother may have so many unbearable habits—so many, i should add—he definitely knew a talent when he saw one."

"I see you're still kind. Always—"

"Interrupting?"

"That too—"

"i guess that's what i'm struggling with."

"You laugh, but... this is important. So, please, quit interrupting m—"

"Okay, fine!"

"Thanks! As i was saying... I have always been weird about expressing feelings—Don't even try. i can just feel you wanting to interrupt—Thing is... I've always wanted to tell you that... you're really important to me."

"Okay, first of, i wouldn't interrupt."

"Yes you would. I felt on your breath."

"Well, that's just weird."

"Not really. I know you pretty well."

"Perhaps..."

"Do you doubt that, huh?"

"Look, i have to go now. We'll talk—"

"Clarissa... wait..."

"What?"

"Did I say something wrong?" "Why ask that?"

"It's just that the conversation was going well, and now, all of a sudden, you need to go. I'm wondering if it's something i said, or—"

"Just stop, please."

"Whoa! There's the tone again."

"i'm only trying to show you that there's nothing wrong. As you keep... insisting. It's Monday—in case you haven't noticed—and, as you know—assuming you remember, of course—i have a job to tend to. That's all."

"Right. You could've just told me that."

"Why do i always have to please you?"

"Please me?"

"Yes. It just seems like it always has to be about you."

"That's not fair."

"Not fair? Seriously?"

"C—"

"Don't C me. You call me that when you're trying to be cute. And...i don't think this is quite the moment for that. You started something... You opened doors that weren't even there. So, i think we should address those things first. Then, we'll see. Don't you think?"

"Maybe. But... you're the one with no time."

"Of course..."

"Look, I'm sorry, Clarissa."

"For what?"

"What do you mean?"

"What exactly are you apologizing for?"

"I don't know. I just—"

"Exactly."

"Didn't mean to upset you. Just wanted to talk, hear your voice, perhaps catch up on things since... I just wanted to, uhm.. I wanted to... I guess wanted to know! you know?"

"i really don't—"

"Clarissa!"

"Look, at this point, i've invested five minutes into this conversation. And, while it's been lovely, i still have to mind my job. Definitely can't stay on the phone so long this early in the morning when clients are trying to find me. They do need me, you know?"

"Would you agree that this is not the first time we've talked while you're at work?"

"i would."

"So?"

"So what?"

"Do you see?"

"Look, i get that you have always been weird about using your words— as you very-well said— but, in this instance... do you think that you could... maybe make an effort?"

"I guess what i'm trying to understand is why is it that suddenly you can't speak with me—"

"i'm sure that's not what i said."

"Okay, you can't speak at work."

"i didn't say that either..."

"Hmm!"

"While i would love to stay here and indulge in this back-and-forth i really can't. i still have meetings to prepare for and a few order things before that. So, i must—"

"Clarissa!"

"When you get the courage to tell me precisely why you called—i see you can still dial number—feel free to call me back."

"C, that's a bit rude. Don't you think?"

"Rude? In the last five or six minutes, you called me unfair and, now, rude. i guess i'm just wondering whether you're able to see yourself just as... well.. as you seem to see me."

"What do you mean?"

"You said you knew me pretty well."

"I don't understand."

"i know, perhaps you could take the time to think about it. i must to go—"

The green did nothing. i wore it because i was told it symbolized new-beginnings. i trusted that. The tight dress did nothing. i wore it hoping that confidence would flood me out. i guess i was wrong on both counts.

The Man i Love calling me, on that day, at that time, that way, it was all downright disconcerting, literally disturbing, irritating.

i couldn't tell whether He didn't see the missed calls or He was just trying to avoid confrontation. The overnice posture, the attempted flattering, the long sentences—yes, even that—The Man i Love was pleasantly of very few words. So, that was out of character.

It is true that sometimes i hated His monosyllabic responses; however, i learned to deal with them a while ago. i knew The Man i Love. i knew Him well. What i didn't know was whatever He was being. The Man i Love sounded cumbersome. i really wasn't one who cared for ambivalence. i trusted He knew that.

Before the clouds veiled the night's final secrets, before she surrendered to the pale radiance of dawn, before the moon and sun met in passing, before nature stirred from its slumber—all was still.

Mr. John, the security guard, caught my eye as i strode through the museum entrance, my silhouette bold and deliberate in the early light. He winked, a small gesture sparked by more than mere beauty—it was the confidence with which i carried each curve, an energy that shimmered around me. Mr. John, with his unremarkable features and unassuming presence, was the one who, in my fractured state, pulled from me a rare, unguarded smile. Somehow, his quiet kindness anchored me in a way i hadn't expected.

But as i slid my phone back into my hand, a question cut through me like a cold blade: why had The Man i Love chosen this exact moment to tear my life apart?

life will bit you down
may bargain your dreams
slaughter your acquittal
but you must persevere

He lowered His voice some more, releasing deep, long, and shameless snorts. He passed on the galling impression that i had, somehow, done something wrong by Him. The Man i Love deflated His core with a silence that imbedded a guilt in me. One that even my most thought-out logic could never egest. i was on the verge of believing in His colorful state of confusion. Thank heavens, i all but recognized the malice in His act of idiocy in the nick of time. His ill inventive answers sounded just like what they were: over-bolded lies. The sadness posed on His declarations was deceit. i saw that in full. i knew Him well, thereon my decision about not swallowing such an appalling performance.

"Can I at least call you back?"

"That's what i just said... isn't it?"

"I'm only making sure," He grumbled.

"Do as you well please. That's how you've always done things. i don't see any reason for you to act any differently now."

"Clarissa—"

"i have to go."

When all was said and done, the Man i Love came to know me completely. And i, now beyond regret, began freeing myself from the shadows he left behind. Mr. John, ever watchful, noticed the scowl etched across my face—a stark and unmistakable mark of displeasure. He was a bold man, but he also understood that i could be dangerously determined when i embraced that edge. Recognizing this, he chose the wiser path, refraining from commenting on the lines of tension creasing one of the smoothest parts of my face. He nodded, a simple gesture that served as a mere acknowledgment, free of judgment and pretense.

With my fitted black dress still sculpting a silhouette reminiscent of the Serra-da-Leba— one of Mother's most breathtaking landscapes—i took myself twelve floors above ground. Once there, i unleashed my frustrations on the papers that had once sat neatly piled on my polished, convertible desk.

Unlike before, it was Him in unrest. Taken back to beautiful moments of ours. He was earnestly pondering upon ways He could leave me in undress. He did so. Not me. He changed at once. As a sign of, what seemed like a groundless epiphany, The Man i Love reminisced about a poem He once mocked:

when you smile
when you cry
when you run miles
when you fly
when it hurts
when that completes
when there're no words
when answers have the birds

                    their songs
                    your thoughts
that's when you know!

when a second is all
when no time is enough
when life is dull
when waiting is tough
when everything is pleasant
when love is present
when the heart burns
when nostalgia reigns
that's when you know!

when the body weakens
when words fade
when pressure deepens
when absence is blade
when all is warm
when they are home
when freedom is right
when they're tight
        their embrace
        your grace
that's when you know!

when songs make sense
when even colors are intense
when poems cause quake
when without them it's ache
when you flare in tears
when you fear
when the entire dream is one
when a person is that
that's when you know!

Outside, in the endless stretch of space above the flower-laden grounds, all appeared as it always had. The night's gentle light surrendered to the sun, casting its golden warmth over freshly cut grass, where morning dew shimmered like embers scattered across the field. Drawing closer to the lawn, the tranquility deepened, a serene dawn settling on all who gathered there.

Children played in the park, their laughter echoing as grandmothers sat anchored to the benches, watching time slip by in the hands of their grandchildren. Around them, others wore their weekday expressions, faces lined with the day's responsibilities. The air carried the familiar scent of a week's end—a mix of weary joy, laughter, and lingering sighs. The mood was one of quiet satisfaction, as bellies emptied of wine, heads cleared of pain, and stomachs freed from their anxious knots. Hangovers, migraines, and stinging nerves—all dissipated.

For every flicker of joy around Him, there was a single heart trembling in silent agony—His. His chest heaved in broken breaths, seized by the fear that he had truly lost me, that i was now beyond His reach.

The Man i Love clung desperately to vivid images of the one He had deceived: me. He saw my hair—luminous, alive. My face—smooth and dark as the ripest plum, my neck—graceful, like Mother's tallest giraffes. He saw my breasts lifted to the sky, my legs, radiant and endless, each step, driven and mighty.

He pictured my laughter, a sound He could no longer hear but still feel, and the strength in my gaze, the quiet fire that had always challenged Him. Every detail, every essence of Mother's daughter, burned into His memory, leaving Him hollow with the unbearable truth: He had lost not only a lover, but the soul He'd once anchored Himself to.

For me, life surged with possibilities once more. Scalding grains of sand wrapped around my toes, while gusts of rebellious wind lashed my face, scrubbing away dried rivers of past tears, smoothing over the flushed peaks of my own allure—the inviting contours i carried, the enticing uplands of my body. My gaze, feverish and alive, devoured everything around me: the people, each vibrating with their own stories. Runners hugged the shoreline, carrying fragile hopes and wearing masks of unsteady poise. Children's screams filled the air—raw, untamed bliss. Young women paraded in featherlight crop tops, sun-drenched skin and belly buttons catching every eye, leaving the elderly stumbling in their wake. Boys strutted in flashy, form-fitting shorts, twerking to the beat of their own egos, each stride lifting the well-worn shapes of their pride. This was life, in all its brazen, chaotic beauty. And every sight, every pulsing rhythm, was a fresh possibility laid bare, daring me to choose.

In retrospect, following the shady call, getting back to work seemed tedious and backbreaking. i was barely able to take myself up to my office. From Mr. John's concealed judgment to the scattered papers across my hundred-square-foot space, the journey was smashing. Every step was a dizzying sensation.

My hair-strings did not just resemble the branches of an imbondeiro tree. They felt just as heavy as the woody perennial plant. Like they had been snowed under a rabble of ambiguous thoughts. Not to mention, if i trusted one thing about The Man i Love, it was His knowledge of how much i didn't care for ambivalence. That's why i questioned His motives for posturing that charade of mixed feelings before my ears.

My shoeprints were soiled with the niff pellet He decided to so selfishly throw at me. Calling me at my weakest, forging covalent bonds, faking affectionate feelings, even forcing passionate reactions. The Man i Love really did a number—with that, then unwanted call. He pushed out of me blows that sent clenches up my spine, filling my arms with cold. My once steady hands suddenly broke out in gooseflesh.

Immediately when the tanned sole of my three-inch pumps stepped on the first tile in my office, i lapsed into an almost mute breakdown. i was again boiling inside. The frowns of desperation returned to veil my colored face.

It was as if i had given up on the idea of pretending strength. Like i would verily embarrass myself amongst my peers, screaming with the boasting of a restive child. At which point, time started dishonoring my hard-attained self-control. Unjustly dragging me back to the customary tormenting illusions. Pulling me into a differing version of that call. Forming a mental image of what would've been my sincere reaction to His tender incentives. An image in which they were explained most convincingly.

The night-full bodycon dress elongated with dark green floral lace met the fountain's edge, escorted by a tickling touch on each of my silky cheeks. Although my tone may have sounded curt to The Man i Love, the feelings inside me were nothing less than life-giving. Screaming out in desperation, wanting to be released, shared with Him: The Man i Love. The man i so deeply loved—day and night, far and near, all or none—the man i still love.

'i have to go—' such was the ending.

Granted The Man i Love was mostly imagining things, that ending made it much more challenging to convince Him otherwise.

i was curt. The rays of my voice were not as caring as in our past exchanges. In all the time i had known this spoiled man, never had i left Him with an elusive silence. Never! Either i'd adorn the ambiance with a close-lipped smile or, The Man i Love would straight-up issue a laugh to dismiss. That's how we would've ended. i should have realized.

i should've known to control my discontent. i should've just indulged Him in a pleasurable conversation like He wanted. An exchange like the ones before. i should've gone back to our past, even if i wanted nothing less. i should've realized the grounds of His frightened state. i could've at least spared Him the disconcert.

Calls unanswered and unreturned. Voice messages ignored. Excessive uneasiness. Cold responses. Dubious disregard of my soul. Ultimately, jitters unexplained. Despite all of that, under no circumstances would i ever—in any way, by any means, for any reason—hurt this man. Never! Therefore, it was on me.

The Man i Love did indicate being sad. Feeling overwhelmed with a bittersweet sensation. He did. So, it was my fault. My own discontent and disbelief notwithstanding, i should never have stooped to His level.

As it stood, the harm in my being was self-inflicted. The tears watering the papers on my desk were, for the first time, of my own making. It was on me to stop them. So i did.

With the very last Kleenex soaked and sealed in my fist, i recalled Mr. Johns' daring wink and reissued the same smile. i decided to return to my self. The daring compliment served me as an inspiring boost. In essence, stripped of any mask and submerged in determination, i decided i had to, somehow, do right by me—favor my existence.

i was done with the last meeting of the day, a few minutes past six. Barely an hour before the sun fell into a slumber.

Restored, i got in my car. The bodycon dress met the snug seats of the lukewarm vehicle, escorted by a flattening touch on each of my silky cheeks. i drove. But, unlike other times, i ended up nowhere.

The sun was wrapped in an orange sky when they both kissed the shivering ocean. The intimacy was staggering. Till then, i had never felt so blest. Life was again overflowing with possibilities. Scalding grains of sand were bathing my toes. Spikes of rebellious winds were punching my face, scrubbing off dry-valleys of gone tears. I was true at last. Acknowledging the new-found possibilities. Throwing my happiness into the air—sharing with all creatures, giving to the unhappy.

life will give
time will charge
to truly value
you will lose

It took some time, but the skies broke open. The sharpest beams I had ever felt swarmed across my window shutters, warming my feet to an awakening. The inner-sphere was awash with hope. With my eyes shown unshut, I dragged out the first lights of the day. I was well aware of my desires. I knew what I wanted, thrill by thrill. Which is why I took my time getting up. I rolled my body over—border to border—until the bed was on fire. My heat was in every stitch of those sheets. As I took my hands to a tour along my frame, artful groans spoke of my frenzy. The Rabbit took care of me in ways I had never dared to allow. Morsels of my pleasure roused the neighborhood and disclosed a new day.

The witching hour washed away by the powers of the blazing star. Distress, despair, dismay—released from my reprieve glands, once and for all. My consort of steps taking their squeaks to new horizons, making lyrical sounds with the freshness of the new-found possibilities. Even the smiles thrown to hail friendly neighbors. All were signs of my revival. A life about me. About my wantings and concerns. After so long, a life engaged in beneficial ventures: all verily beneficial to me. The day was as new as I felt.

To celebrate this newfound zeal, i slipped into the floral-print jeans that had been buried in the neat corners of my closet. Yellow symbolized happiness and hope, both of which i was brimming with, so the yellow chiffon blouse with short sleeves felt like the perfect choice. For the finishing touch, i elevated myself another two inches—not to walk, but to stride boldly in five-inch corset heels designed to command attention. Fear was nowhere in sight. That's why the heels were apple-red, echoing the flowers on the pants, vibrant against the backdrop of neither yellow nor green. With my look flawlessly assembled, i headed to work, ready to own every step.

"Wow, Ms. Mixima, you look dazzling!

"Already told you can call me by my first name. And, thank you! You're too kind.

"Sorry, Clarissa. But, yes, you do look amazing. On different note, thought: I don't think that Mr. Frank can be too kind today.

"What? What are you talking about?"

"I'm sure he'll fill you in. He told me to send you to his office once you got here."

"Oh, okay. Thanks, Anne."

As i took the files from my secretary, a shadow of doubt crept in, and i couldn't help but wonder how my day might soon unravel. Frank wasn't just a visionary; he was the kind of boss who valued connection and harmony above all. Company cohesion was his cornerstone. Anne knew that too. So, for her to hint otherwise, i knew it had to be something serious, something not to ignore.

"Argh, good, you're here, finally."

"Why the frustration? I'm on time!"

"Well, today that's not enough."

"So I was told. What's going on?"

"Email these people. Thank them for their help last week. Reinforce the idea that we can always use them around here. Send shirts or something. Do whatever you need."

"Is that all?"

I realized that wasn't exactly my job, and I wasn't even at the event in question. But, our Volunteer Coordinator was on her leave, and everybody was pitching in, so I didn't mind.

"I wish that was all, Clarissa. There's also a delegation from the MMBP coming—

"Oh, yes. The Museum of Music of the Bantu people. I saw that on your schedule."

"Well, that's just it. I can't really attend the meeting. So, I need you to cover it for me.

"But Frank, I'm not prepared."

"There isn't much to prepare for. You completed that program on African Studies. Not to mention, you love music—"

"Yes, but—"

"Clarissa, I really can't debate this right now. I still have lots to do. Send the emails; get with Anne and prepare for the meeting. You can also make use of my secretary, she knows everything I was planning on doing."

"But, Frank—"

"The delegation should get here in two hours. I have to go—"

I knew those words very well. I've used them before. I understood the need for them. Therefore, I concealed my frowns of outrage and begun working. I decided that not even Frank's bad-mood would ruin the day for me.

Parading my floral jeans around the office, I put in my best work performance yet.

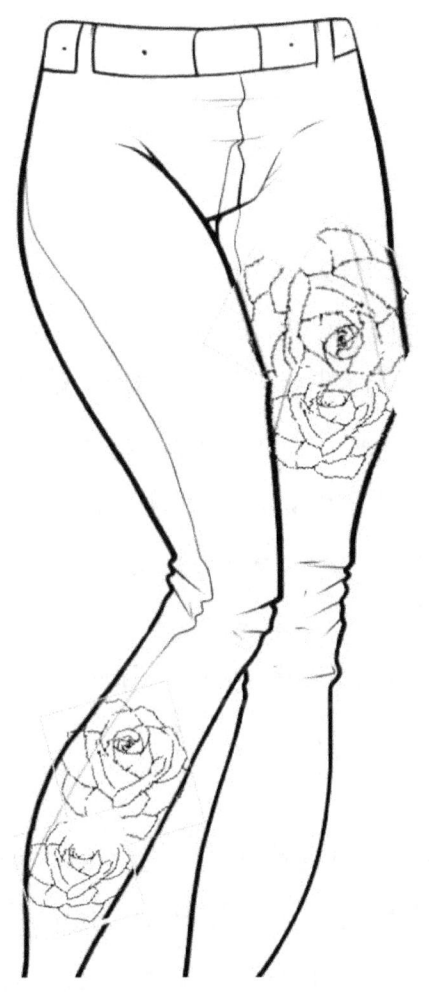

It took a while, but eventually I was able to catch my breath. For a second—a very brief second—I allowed myself to get lost. I placed my silky cheeks on the swivel desk chair and rolled to the hundred-foot glassy-wall behind me. The night was evident. The cold could've been felt through the synchronized dancing of the trees aligned along the square. I knew the air was fresh by watching the smiley sniffs on the faces of the distracted footgoers. It was like the flowers' odors were piercing their insides, pushing out blows that sent glares to their eyes. Even the way they were walking was a sign of how delightful the evening was. I saw it. I felt it. And, the deep breath I drew was to take it all in: the night upon me!

In the end, i didn't just have a productive meeting—I had a productive day. Emails were sent, and my inbox was cleared of those nagging blue dots. Replies were given, letters read, and new connections were made. i even managed to finalize negotiations on a collection we'd been pursuing for ages. It felt like a small victory, a reminder of the strength i could summon when i needed it most. By the time the streetlights were the only glow illuminating the city, every task had been completed.

"Ahh... So glad the meeting went well. Can't imagine this place without you." Frank's face was relaxed at last, and his body expression more welcoming.

"Oh, but I'm sure you can."

"What are you talking about?"

"It's just that... the way you treated me today—"

"Ahh! I'm so sorry, Clarissa. I think I've just been—"

"In over your head?"

"Yes. See what I'm saying? This place would be a mess without you. I'd be a mess!"

"Don't even think twice about it—"

"Seriously, thank you, C."

i wasn't ready. My mouth abstained from unlocking. My eyes widened. My body bristled and froze. All the while i assured myself that wasn't one of those moments. But the truth is, it had been a while since anyone called me that. Since i had to think about it. About Him. So, that little letter threw me off.

"Are you okay? Did I say something—"

"Oh, don't worry. I'm... I'm totally fine. Maybe just a little tired. It's been a day!"

"Yes, it has."

Frank wasn't just a boss. He was a good friend. Although the other late nights were less forced, we had been there before: deep sights, sad stories, a glass or two of wine, at times, even tears—with and without big laughs. We had also shared out heart aches. That's how I knew He would pick up on my hesitation to answer his question. He'd know.

"I really don't know what I would've done without you today. So, thank you!"

"Don't mention it!"

"Like you not mentioning what's really bothering you? And don't even try to deny it. We'll talk about this later. For now: go home, deep your amazing self into a bath, have a glass of wine, and enjoy a restful sleep."

As Frank uttered those words and left my office, I realized he was right. In fact, he always was. I just couldn't bring myself to agree with him then. My heart grew strained.

"What are you still doing here?"

"You're still here, Ms. Mixima—sorry, Clarissa. Do you need anything else?"

"I need you to go home to your beautiful family. That's all I need from you right now."

"Now who's being too kind?"

"Well—"

"You still have those emails to send. The ones Mr. Frank mentioned earlier—"

"Damn, you're right. I'll take care of it."

Dear change-makers,

Thank you so much for sharing your time and talents with us. We appreciate you more than words can describe. With your participation in the benefit concert, we were able to raise close to a million dollars that will fund art programs in destitute communities. We hope to keep counting on your support.

Sincerely,

Clarissa Mixima
Museum of African Art
Exhibit Designer & Art Curator

Even without the promise of thank-you shirts, the email was as sweet as it was short. With that, I pressed 'send.' Things got real' twisted after that. I took a second look at one of the names that appeared on the list. A hard look, just to make sure. Frankly, had I known, I wouldn't have signed my name so boldly.

if resilience remains
life is still in you
if fighting pains
then you know it's true

For the newest chapter of my life, i was thinking: erase every message, empty out the entire call history, and delete all of the emails. Put on the shortest dazzling skirt nicely folded in the symmetry of my drawers, go out with sassy Becky—preferably somewhere out of town—and lose control. i would carry brightness of my own making, even with my wrinkles outed. i would wear the most cunning face. My confidence would forever be unshaken, and my fears would never be greater than my ambitions. i would be the one unleashing my flowers, Rabbit or not. i would fear no deception. i would enjoy myself, making my own happiness bloom. Every thing would be evidence of my revival.

Instead of merely gluing my luscious bootie on the warmness of a swivel task chair, flooding my desk with old and exhausted tears. Instead of spending my days hoping for its nimble end and my nights mourning an undeserving love, begging for death. Instead of putting myself through such denigrating circumstances, i would restart. i would adopt another. If not, i would at least revisit a happier moment. Maybe Phil could be such a moment. Not T, surely not him. He could never be that. Oddly enough, Matthew was more likely to be so, a moment of pure delight, since that's all he ever was, a moment.

Despite being a good and delicate man—a caring man—T was a past i had decided to leave there. Phil, on the other hand, was only someone i once knew. Meanwhile, Matthew was undoubtedly a commendable odyssey. The most haunting memory i ever had. He was one of those guys to whom i'd never allot a second glance, despite the glasses, which, i admit, showed some kindness to his beauty. He wasn't tall enough—not as tall as The Man i Love, not even as tall as T. He wasn't high in stature, cloaked with savory meat, very-well built; that wasn't him. Still, for my maze, it was him who riled me up. Only him! i blindly allowed his entry into my nether region.

The night was stripped of its stars, as i was of my joy. It lay silent, much like i did, with barely a whisper from the rain to disturb the stillness. Nature slept soundly, oblivious to the shadows haunting me. i struggle to remember the precise moments that led me to despair, but i can never forget what followed. It clings to me like a permanent tattoo.

My tall, curved frame yielded to him—Matthew—a short, unassuming man with an uninspired presence. Perhaps it was because my eyes were closed, perhaps because my thoughts were elsewhere, or maybe he simply knew his craft too well. With the touch of his hands, the insertion of his fingers, he drew out sounds from me that echoed like thunder. That was all. And perhaps that was best, as i'm not sure i could have handled more. Up to that point, i had never felt my own warmth so deeply, so densely, so... dripping. As things are, i fear i never will again. Matthew marked himself in my memory in ways no one else ever has.

Setting aside his plain appearance, he possessed an uncanny skill. His lips were capable, his knowledge supreme. i still recall the feeling of our juices mingling, his mouth tracing a path over my most sensitive places in blissful combinations. Matthew gave me something unforgettable—not my first, but undeniably the best. From my earlobe to my neck, from there to my nipples, until he finally lingered at the apex of my desire, revealing parts of me i hadn't even known were waiting to be found.

Instead of wasting my time grieving, i relived the most extraordinary event of my life. i felt Matthew afresh. i felt him in me. Succeeding so many unsavory groans, i felt undeserving of The Big O. Not me. i couldn't have that. i was one of those women who just couldn't achieve—i thought. That was until Matthew, the short formed fellow who made me feel otherwise. Disgracefully, the thought was as rushed as my first squirt. Soon after, it was Him again in my mind—The Man i Love.

He insinuated Himself into my mind. After a second look into those names, i was again baffled. Only then, i was ready to avert more. The Man i Love would not have me back. One of us would expire before that happened. And, i was sure it wouldn't be me.

i wondered why He was at the museum at all. i wondered about His intentions.

i remember one of the conversations i had with Him. Can't make up what actually led us to the topic, but i know we reached it.

"What would you do if you knew your partner cheated on you?"

For all i know, either one of us could've asked that question. That's unimportant now! i couldn't see His face, but i knew the dimples weren't there. Instead, i felt the frowns. i knew The Man i Love like no one else. i knew Him well. His body went from prostrating to taking a chair. It wasn't anger. The thought of facing such upheaval left Him uncomfortable. Of course He knew i'd never do this scummy thing to Him. And i did assure Him of that. With me, The Man i Love would never feel such ghastly pain. Knowing so, He explained:

"I would kill both of you—of them... I mean. I do not forgive betrayal. Never!"

i wasn't surprised in the least.

To this i can attest: The Man i Love had always been rather reserved, pretty careful, and pleasantly of very few words. High in stature, cloaked with savory meat, marked by fullness of flavor. He wore the most cunning face. It bore a downiness like no other. The well-fitted and grand figure He owned had always been the secret ingredient for the best hugs. i'm yet to meet a more lulling hugger. The Man i Love was all of those things. He was perfect in His imperfections; sensitive, strong, and well-spirited. Altogether true. To that i do attest. Alas, He was also unduly proud. Hence my tranquility toward His somewhat extreme reaction. Besides, He often wore His I-want-things-my-way face. i knew it well. Moreover, i did appreciate His possessive personality. The change in His tone. The frowns on His face. The keen tingles all over His body. It'd all be rather provoking.

If i told people i had missed not one, but multiple calls from The Man i Love before these complications; they probably wouldn't believe. But i did. Of course i never did that purposefully and i hated every single time it had to happen; however, it is still did happen. Never had i experienced Him so out of sorts. The change in His tone. He'd speak like each voiced word was a sword gored into his heart. The frowns on His face. He'd enhance His appearance with lines that screamed His rage. The keen tingles all over His body. i could never forget those. Sometimes i'd feel his cold. i do have to say, despite the purple prose, i appreciated His implicit declarations.

One instant of the past still lingers in the clutter of my mind. i was returning His call.

"Oh... You do have my number. That's good to know."

It wasn't what He said. Not at all. i could very well live with that. It was the flustered tone. While, nine times out of ten, i'd appreciate the words He wasn't intrepid enough to articulate, i had that one time to remind me of the woman I was. Which was never one to allow insolence—however gallant. So, He got to know me better. With all speed, i set Him straight. Empathetically, of course since mine was love never to hurt.

"It's not only that you missed the call, it's that you took forever to return it and, on top of that, your number became unavailable. I was worried, that's all."

"i do understand," that was my full response. At that point, The Man i Love was surely familiar with the implications.

It was never the three-word term out of His skillful mouth. The Man i Love knew all the ways to flex His mouth just enough to steer clear of commitment. i didn't mind the chase. It made things more interesting.

This is who He was. i knew Him well. Therefore, His response to the question was unsurprising. Nevertheless, i repeated His answer back to Him, just to double check.

"Wow! You'd kill us?—them... i mean," i knew what i was doing. It was no mistake.

"Absolutely. No doubt. I do not forgive betrayal," The Man i Love replicated His answer, word-for-word.

"Huh, interesting."

love will always come ashore
you must defend your heart
even when ending is the cure

He had to answer my calls or at least return them in a timely fashion. He couldn't just call and play absent-minded with me. One thing i knew about Him is that He was never such a thing. The Man i Love wasn't forgetful in the least. That i knew for sure. Just like i knew it wasn't fair to expect from others what one wasn't willing to match. He had to know that. Furthermore, The Man i Love had to know i'd be biting my nails until an explanation invaded my ears or, better yet, until it came into my sight. i'm sure He was aware of the confusion that remained following our last telephonic exchange. It wasn't right for The Man i Love to leave me wondering about the blistering voice i heard.

That said, i feel betrayed. i feel cheated.

It isn't just the endless questions or the doubts that cloud my mind. It's not just the memories that strike my core or the delirium that consumes me. It's not simply the weakness flooding my bones or the uncertainty that leaves me on the edge of collapse. No. It's something more, something deeper. It's not just the emotional turbulence, the relentless mood swings. It's everything i've yet to release, all the unspoken words knotted within me.

i was never one to distrust people at first glance. Not until He made me so. i was never this guarded, this stoic. My heart used to be visible from miles away—that was who i was. The Man i Love took that from me. He dismantled my peace, my clarity. It was Him. Of this, i am sure.

i might still be uncertain of the call-girl's identity, yet, if i were to truly listen to Him, i would have grounds to erase them both from my heart.

The Man i Love did leave me in pieces. He wrecked our memories. He got them dirty. Every single time i went back and thought of ways He could've been deceiving me. Every single time i doubted His honesty. Every time i considered that i could've been misjudging my confidence, pride, and my ability to recognize a decent person. What's worse, every time i questioned my reasons for continuing that challenging relationship. Even my disconcert over a name on a list, annoyed me beyond words. It had already been too long, i should've been able to keep on. So, yes, every time my mind got flooded with those baneful thoughts, i felt a sword being gored into my core. It was all His fault.

The Man i Love was cruel. Maybe just that one time, but still, He was. Becoming aware of His double-dealing was hands down one of the hardest things i had ever faced. He pulled the reality rug right under me. There're no ifs ands or buts about it. That's the truth.

We had built something as rare as it was beautiful, a bond two souls might create once in a lifetime. The comfort we found in each other was unparalleled, the trust we shared everything. It showed in the warmth of my cheeks, in the quiet depth of His dimples. We had it, that connection people dream of.

But now, i was lost, with no idea what to think or do. Until he finally explained, betrayal hadn't even crossed my mind. The possibility seemed unthinkable; he wasn't like that. Not the man i loved. And yet, he'd acted as if he was. The rare, fragile trust between us had shattered in a single, careless moment, leaving me grasping for answers, clinging to the pieces of who we once were.

"i love you, but i don't forgive betrayal," i whispered, the words hollow yet heavy, falling between us like a finality neither of us could take back.

i would love Him first. The Man i Love would finally have full access to me, and i'd let Him in completely. There'd be no waiting, no futile hope for some childishly romanticized moment. We would create our own. But not in the back of a Camaro or Mustang—that wouldn't work. As much as i wanted to recreate those daring tales of nineteen-sixty-nine, i'd need the comfort of four walls for it to feel right. Yet, none of those walls could be mine; i would still, however shamelessly, want a chance to keep going, to love again.

A hotel room would be too obvious, incriminating me far too soon, so that was out of the question. And bringing anyone else in? Foolishness. If there's one thing true about me, it's that, feelings aside, i do my best to avoid being reckless—or so i like to think. But perhaps i was already teetering on the edge of risk, knowing that to love Him was to gamble with my very heart. Whatever the case, i'd have to face this choice alone. No doubt i would.

Even if, in the end, i lost my right to freely enjoy the vastness of the skies. My opportunity to visit the places of our dreams, if for nothing else, to honor Him—The Man i Love. Even if that was the very last thing i could ever do without the shadowing of armed forces and the quashing of an orange suit, i would do it!

i would happily give my life away if that meant the return of my sanity, the advent of happiness. One that was my own. i would also do it if the end result was a world-altering orgasm by The Man i Love. My second, if not my last. An excitement that drained the life out of me. i craved for it at length. i wanted nothing more. The Man i Love knew that.

All of our phone conversations were filled with details of an encounter just as fervid. The texts too. i knew what He wanted just like He was acquainted with my thirst. So, before i took Him at His words, i would love

Him. i would use all of my strength to create a striking end. One that lasted long enough to stay forever affixed to my memories. One i could happily relive even if unjustly kept in a dark six-by-eight stall. i would give myself something legendary. i deserved it. After everything, it was only right. The Man i Love would have all of me. And i would get His life-seeds—not to bloom, just to feel. To mark a moment, our moment at last. A full one.

The dancing butterflies in the grave of my desires would be gone. The elated thrills would breach my skin, enlarging my pores. The blindness gracing my flushed face would reveal every single one of my suppressed oomphs. Our dreams. The fiery cravings we shared. The Man i Love would have His stout life-providing pipe deep in my warmth. i would scream. My life-sucking engine would douse the fleshy part of His ear. With the wildest acts of my mouth, He would know of my urges. Or part of it. His left-hand locking mines on the ridge of my crown-bun. The insistence between His athletic legs. His ins manipulating the outs. The pressure. The insertion. i would love Him for all of it! The Man i Love would denote the strongest feeling of emotional attachment. He would love me like His life depended on it.

i didn't know anything about the poor fool He was equally deluding—if there was even one. She could've very well be His sister. Her voice was scorching, that was true. i knew nothing of her reasons for infringing on the privacy of The Man i Love and addressing me with such a high-pitched tone. My rage toward her had to be further deliberated. But, no matter the findings, i would defend my heart, shielding it with His very own words:

'I would kill both of them.'

*it will hurt like life
but it'll be as antidotal as death*

Spongy looking spheres of aromatic nothing covering my unclad body as it sinks in gauzy liquid tinged pink by soothing bombs. That's how i would start readying myself. The Man i Love would get His wishes. Funge would be prepared ahead of time. i'd make it softer than usual so that time didn't harden it as brutally as it did my heart. i'd consider Fish Stew or Chicken Yassa as compliment, but would never make either since they're both too greasy. My desire would be to introduce The Man i Love to the best Mother had to offer while impelling His passion. Hard boiled eggs and long sausages swimming in boiling spicy sauce would be just that, an aphrodisiac and sign of my pride.

My glass would be filled to capacity all day long. The Chardonnay would accompany me through every corner of the house—from stove to bathtub, from mine to the dining room—i'd refill my courage with every single pouring; prepare myself for the looming end.

The rich, deliciously scented blend of evening primrose, sweet almond, apricot kernel, and jojoba oils would sweeten the cascade on my body as it penetrated my pores, leaving my skin ready for His touch. The Man i Love would drown in goosebumps from the second He laid His thirsty eyes on me. With my paths polished and fragranced, i'd slowly put my meaty legs in the holes of a floral lace thong, allowing the bonded hem to caress me. It's waist would divide my figure just right, boldly highlighting my indigenous curves.

My round-shaped horned breasts would be well guarded behind the matching floral brassiere. They'd both be white. The Man i

Love had it as His favorite color, so i'd honor that. The lace garter belt would rest just above my navel, allowing its strings to tightly halt the back seam stockings. For my final liaison with The Man i Love i would be breathlessly armored.

My feet would be lewdly adorned with heels high enough to land my ears on His shoulders amidst our embrace. The only color on my square heels sandals would be in its insole. Yes, it would be white—i could pass for an angel, were it not for the sinful desires flooding my mind. The ankle strap would be transparent, just like the rest of the heel. The buckle would be as tight as He'd later be.

My first choice would be to steer clear of dresses completely. With a racy apron and matching gloves the whole thing would have been just as i once dreamed. However, i would rather The Man i Love didn't run straight for dessert. He earned the right to a delicious last meal!

i remember the second day my randy eyes encountered His juicy figure. Once in a while, the episode still fills my mind. With a vibrant three-sixty spin, The Man i Love made me fly. What i remember now is the little black dress. His eyes lost on me as He spotted me for the very first time. The Man i Love lifted me up and arranged me on His wide shoulders forming, with my hairless body, a hug meant to smash bones. Before i knew, my legs were floating shy, parallel to His. i went places only one of us will ever go. i wanted that, and much more.

For the occasion, the dress would be as captivating as ever—perhaps even more—but it would be white. Yes, like clouds, pure yet dangerously alluring. The Man i Love deserved to part with a vision of ethereal allure, a face He'd never forget, seared into His memory as something almost too perfect to touch. i'd fulfill His deepest desires, leaving no corner of His imagination unexplored, no fantasy unlit.

The Classic Glam dress would rest just above my knee, grazing the spot where it begins to bend, though i wouldn't make that move too soon. The sleek bodycon skirt would feature a slit along the left thigh, rising just high enough to tease, to spark a thrill in any gaze. Off-the-shoulder with short sleeves, a bodice traced with delicate princess seams, it would reveal only hints, seducing with restraint, making him crave what lay just out of reach. The Man i Love would be forced to conjure the satisfaction of His deepest curiosities, every dark indulgence and wild desire mercilessly painted in His mind, each thought edging toward madness.

Through it all, i'd hold His gaze, a knowing smile lingering on my lips—the kind that spoke of our shared secrets, our unspoken vows. And even if giving Him this vision broke me, even if it was a final act of surrender, The Man i Love would walk away with exactly what He deserved.

"You are a vision."

"I should be. After all I had to do—"

"I'm sure it didn't take too much effort. You've always been this beautiful. It's just that... for some reason... it all feels enhanced today. It's like I am seeing you for the very first time. Like I'm smelling you for the..." The Man i Love would grow silent precisely in the weakest spot of my neck just as He settled my cushions down on His hard-felt thighs. There would be no doubt about His leg days. i would know it for sure.

"Will we just dance all night? I did spend all day cooking for you," it wouldn't be out of anger, rather an excruciating craving.

"It does smell delicious. But not as delicious as you do right now. If it were up to me, yes. We would spend the entire night dancing. Clarissa Mixima, I'm happy here—"

"Just dancing?"

"Well, since you asked—"

"Yes..."

"We could go straight to dessert."

"Huh..."

"Wouldn't you like that?"

The Man i Love would have no idea that my smug face would be the result of my surprise. My whisperings wouldn't cease as a result of anger, no. i'd be faced with the fact that the night was going just as i had planned.

"But i did all of this for you though," I'd turn my head to the side, bringing attention to the decorated and well-stocked table. With His left hand still engraved in my back, The Man i Love would use His right to carefully place my left legs on the ground. Then, with both hands around my waist, i'd be brought up in a smothering embrace. His grip would be imprinting—only my dress would hide it.

"I never said I wouldn't eat it. You have no idea how much I want to—"

"But I'm taking about the food," a smile would reveal my suspicions about His true desires.

"I'm talking about that, too."

"Too? What else are you taking about?"

"I think you know—"

"Well, if—"

"But if you don't, I'd happily show you after this dance."

"Then dance we shall..."

The Man i Love would have no need to lower the sleeves of my dress when branding my shoulders with His lips. No. They would already be bare and ready for His touch.

Bruna Tatiana's hit "Amo-te" would be the one embellishing the background. i would never not show Him my Mother. Never. That was the task that had long been sealed on my subconsciousness. It functioned as my sixth sense. Everything i did had to reflect Mother.

He would have no idea as to how to move His body. But it wouldn't take long for Him to understand that He actually didn't have to.

"That's not how they do it in Angola. Put your hands here," i'd instruct Him.

Instead of allowing Him to spread them like we were dancing Tango, i'd take them both and lock them up on my lower back. Just as He shook with uncertainty, i'd hold them again and place them at my meridian. The Man i Love would be at border of my both breeches—exactly were the mound starts.

"Right here," i'd say.
"Mm!"

i'd grab Him by His neck. It would look like He was a hanger, and i, the dress that'd fit nowhere else. i'd be exactly where i wanted to be, on His shoulders, amidst that embrace. My region would touch His just enough to cause a stir in His gut. That, coupled with the slowly and melodic rotation of both my nates, The Man i Love would know i was always more than He could ever handle.

"What's this song saying?"

"Are you sure that's what you wanna discuss right now? Lyrics?" Sure, i didn't want to tell Him that the song said exactly what i had been saying all that time. i also refused to be the one influencing His declaration of love.

"No! Not really. I only wanted to see if it's at all related to what i'm feeling."

"I see! And what are you feeling?"

"Honestly, i'd rather show you—"

"Right now?"

"Don't think I can wait."

do as if you'd no longer stay
so that when you actually go
you have no regrets to allay

The Man i Love wouldn't say a word, but His hand behind my neck would be a question i'd hear in its loudest. A jumbled kiss would be my consent. Then, we'd both lay our eyes to rest. However, not the eternal one just yet. The stockings would be the first pieces to go. They'd be thrown somewhere behind the sofa. The dress would follow in no time. The Man i Love would remove it with frisky toothing. He'd start by leaving my big toe, as soaked as it would be, then He'd go up. Planting kisses and dragging His tongue throughout my leg. As the warmth came out my entrance, He'd know it was time to undress. So, with groping bites, The Man i Love would remove both my dress and thong.

"Tell me what you want," He'd say.

"Mmm, i think you already know!"

"Still... I want to hear you say it"

"I want you..."

"You do?"

"Yes! I want all...of you."

"And where do you want me?"

i'd grab His head like one would grab a snake—right at its fleshy neck, squeezing it with my fist. His last question would come from the pressure of my grip. He'd feel as though i was drawing the life out of Him, though i wouldn't—not yet. As i pulled its tip closer to my flash point, The Man i Love would seize my hands, guiding them to the north-end of my zipper. With His palms beneath me, lifting me effortlessly, He'd throw me into the air. My landing would be warm and perfectly tight, fitting into Him like a crew slipping seamlessly into its nut, held in an electric, unspoken understanding.

With His index now tied in, motionless, The Man i Love would make His way to the bedroom. He'd not only be struck by a mild smell of lavender, but also the white all around. Thereon, as His muscles uncoiled, emphasizing His desires and their might, The Man i Love would realize fathom heaven. Sadly, even though He'd reach such a moment, i'd already be at a point of no return.

"Mhm. Mm... Mm..."
"Are you okay?"
"I'm perfect!"
"Yes, you are."

There wouldn't be much else to say. My vented moanings would be just the right fuel for The Man i Love. With each passionate notch, He would know of all my wantings.

He wouldn't release me on the bed, no. Those white sheets would remain untouched for the time being. Instead, my silky cheeks would touch-down in the divan. My rinsing would take place there. The Man i Love would take His tongue to the depths of my Mother's daughters, with no intension of returning.

The base of His taste-goblet way at the bottom of my groin. Completely soaked. The Man i Love slowly moving His head upwards from base to crown, reaching my stirred love-button. Even though He'd be going slower than a chameleon, i wouldn't dare remember that funge tasted better warm. i would choose to mull over my flavors in His mouth.

At the turn of each minute, my heart would jump out of my chest, allowing Him to anticipate my spasms, kiss my flower and gauge my reaction. The first session would end with a pleasureful scream and a failed attempt to escape. The Man i Love would sit me up, gather my neck and bend it with a kiss.

His lips would loosen their grip with every milder contraction. A still-touch on my neck with each one. The Man i Love would prolong the moment just by being playful enough with His very accommodating mouth. i would kiss Him back. i'd put my hands back on His neck and every kiss from then on would be a telepathic thank you.

"Will you tell me what you want?"
"I have it. It's you on my arms."
"Yah? Then let me reinforce that."

i would stretch my legs behind His back, like a juicy gossip. Opening it wide enough for an insertion while still tightening for easy maneuvers—painful ins, heavenly outs. i'd go back to His burly neck. Squeezing it with my fist. Grabbing it like a hanger that has just found its ultimate dress. The Man i Love would be brought back to me with the weakening of my hands in the back of His sapient head. We would lock eyes. A drawn out yet closed smile would be a sign for both of us.

i would place both my arms behind my back, parallel to my cheeks. The Man i Love would make His follow. His embrace would be the most beautiful and priceless item i would ever wear. Berita's "Ndiceli'ikiss" would have reached its bridge when i'd finally let out another piercing scream. The Man i Love would know not to stop—actually, He'd know to do just the opposite. No one knew me better. No one could anticipate my needs quite like He did. No one understood the lust in my eyes disguised as mere radiance. None, but The Man i Love. With that said, it was clear that no one but Him would understand me placing my hands in his button's heart and giving it one last massage. He'd know what i needed. He'd pull me up, throw me on the bed and give me one last angry push, putting in completely, as if willfully tearing me up.

It would be my deep groan that'd bring down both our gasps and implant smiles on our faces.

"Are you okay?" He'd ask again. Then, with a different reason in mind.
"I am perfect," i'd sprout rainbows.
"Yes... you definitely are." That I would hear from him

i would know there would be no point in being shy. The Man i Love had already been in me. However, i couldn't help but hide myself behind a closed-eye smile.

"Hey! Look at me." As He held my chin on His hand, He'd pull His lips closer to mine and give a kiss that'd trigger others. With the cold approaching our bare trunks, The Man I Love would pull up the covers, keeping our warmed bodies hidden from the sonic rays of Ayanda Jiya. At that point, He'd have reached

Mother's southernmost area. i'd be relieved to know that it had taken one passionate night to introduce The Man i Love to the entire extension of my Mother. But there'd be more!

"Is this the plan?"

"Mm! It could be."

"Could it?"

"Yes! But, you do want us to enjoy the delicious meal you spent all day preparing—" The Man i Love wasn't one to forget—"Truth is: you took the life out of me—" He'd add.

"Not quite yet. But, it was a marvelous beginning," The Man i Love wouldn't make out my sly smile. He'd get lost in my groans.

"Huh?" A question with fear.

"Oh, nothing! Let's not rush," i'd look at Him, fondle His face and release a smile.

*the fog may conceal the powder, but
the hand never forgets having held the gun*

The Man i Love would dearly look at me, fondle my face, and embed a kiss between my brows making me sprout a rainbow from my cheeks. This would be the last time my randy eyes would encounter His juicy figure. It'd be the first and only day we'd enjoy ourselves with all desires we ever kept in. We'd both finally live the most-awaited moment of our sinful lives. We'd shamelessly expose our cravings, free ourselves from all repressing rules; from dread and idle shyness.

"I adore touching what's mine," The Man i Love would declare.—A wave of chills would unveil my frailness.—"Now that you are mine, I intend to touch every inch of you."

The gleam in my eyes would be one of pure, unbridled satisfaction. Watching my moistened body leave warm traces on the cloud-like silk would be all the sign He'd need. In that moment, The Man i Love would feel like GOD. And by my seventh release, He'd let Himself rest.

With my damp neck cradled in His arms, we'd slip into dreams that would never come to pass: Him lost in what might have been, and i in what could have.

Using the same fingers that had just drawn every sound from me, i would carefully unwind myself from His embrace. His strong, sculpted arms—the ones he so confidently showed off in fitted V-necks—would settle onto the soft comfort of my Angel-Sleeper. The Man i Love would look as He always did in sleep, like a child whose peace was anchored by a single person. And in that moment, i would be that person, willingly and fully. Never would i dare to be, or do, anything else.

With only the prints of my toes being left behind, i'd take myself to drain my sins away. The shower would be long, but not so long that it awakened The Man i Love. i'd still have to re-heat our food and make sure everything was still in place. It wouldn't be wise to go back to crazy-wild love making, regardless of how much of Him i itched for.

The water would still be running through my extension. No towel needed. My body deserved more than to be kept. Just as wet as before, i'd tiptoe to the kitchen and sit His last meal on well-adjusted blue flames. i would wear an apron though. i would never cook naked.

"What're you doing?" The Man i Love would ask.

"I think you know, luv." "Why don't you come here?"

"Again?!"

The Man i Love would understand that, in my tone, was not a disapproval. Rather a playful way of leading Him to exactly where i'd want to be: back in His arms.

"Yes, again," he'd answer; already with His arms wrapped around my shoulders and His lips shocking against my neck in pleasure.

The Man i Love and i would both notice His nothing little dragon firing up extensively making me crazily ready. Our eyes would both open, and we would know that we were both naked. However, it wouldn't be shame guiding us, quite the opposite.

The Man i Love would bend me over at the counter and do what He always did well. i don't know how, but i wouldn't get burned. The savory dripping in my lower extremities would inspire The Man i Love. He'd lift my right leg up and place it on the cold granite.

With His right hand near my navel, The Man i Love would pull me closer; lower me down with His left hand on my back; and spread me out with both His feet. He would be all in.

For my frustration, the timer would go off, snapping us back for a brief moment. Not that The Man i Love would mind. With a few playful paddles, He'd turn me over and press a kiss to my lips—a kiss that would feel like a journey on its own.

i would look at Him with a hunger that could never be sated, and He'd gaze back at me like i was everything He'd ever wanted. My entire body would shine with a smile. He'd trace His hand from my cheek to my palm, lingering, His smile a clear invitation. His fingers would only gradually slip away, as if savoring each second of touch.

Then, i'd set a table for two, slip off my apron, and dash to the shower on my toes, anticipation sparking with each step.

This time we would attire ourselves: An extra-large shirt posing as a habit on my sinful body, and a pair of slim-short-shorts nicely highlighting His well-rounded sloped behind.

The lack of underwear would have left us both vulnerable. Swallowing dribble like we were facing a nice medium rare grilled steak. Me, losing my mind over His bulky package. The Man i Love, drowning in sweet vaginal mist. Releasing warning stares.

Despite our apparently uncontrollable urges, we would make use of the nicely set table and fill our bellies with delicious food. Each empty returning fork would be a question or an elated smile.

"Mmmm, this is delicious. What is it?"
"Hm... Let's see: these are... very hard... boiled eggs and lo-o-o-o-ng sausages in spicy tomato sauce."

"What about this?"

"Ahh, this is funji. Yellow corn flower, boiled and... pounded just hard enough into a dough-like consistency. Like it?"

"Like it?! Love it!"

The Man i Love would not notice the sauce escaping from the corner of His mouth. Or maybe He would.

"Why are you smiling so suspiciously?"

"I'm not," the smile would get wider.

"Yes, you are! Do i have something on my face," He'd then ask.

i would look at The Man i Love like i could read His nutsiest thoughts. With my hand wrapped around His neck, i would pull Him close. Not long after that, the rug of my mouth would leave it's marks all over His face. i'd get down to His neck and slowly spell a kiss or two. As slow as a kiss can be delayed. His shoulders would be a way to get down low. i would even start on His chest, but the taste stuck on my mouth would remind me that the hunger was physical too.

"I'm glad you love it," i'd say.
"You really went all out."
"Oh, you just wait."
"There's more?"

The Man i Love would quickly place an overwhelmed expression over His gaze.

"You don't think you deserve more?"
"I don't know," He'd answer. Like there was nothing to add. Like He knew it already.
"Then, let me tell you."

i would get up, go to the fridge and get back to The Man i Love with two bowls of múkua ice cream. One of them would have the bane. Something i knew He had never seen, never tried. For Him, that would be the ultimate trip through Mother, through me!

All too often, The Man i Love would overlook important things. That's who He was. i knew that about Him, hence my confidence that He would never notice my poison-ring. Maybe He'd think it was just another way to impress Him, or He wouldn't actually see it. In any case, it would finally be put to use. i would empty out the hinged-chamber in the bowl intended for Him. i would believe i could easily tell them apart.

"Here, my luv."
"Wow, I don't deserve you."

We would simultaneously stare into each other's eyes and release a silent laugh confirming what was just said. We'd know it to be true. However, neither i nor The Man i Love would care to address it.

Spoon after spoon, death would seep into His insides. i'd place my manicured fingers— just two, resting gracefully on each other—on the silver handle of the curved utensil. With each slow, deliberate "airplane," i would guide the cold descent through His throat, a delicate ritual of demise. The Man i Love would swallow each creamy drop, each slick mouthful dissolving against the pink of His tongue, lingering for just a second before another followed.

He'd savor each icy gulp, each of my soft smiles that accompanied them. Every spoonful, every gentle insertion, would be at my command. i knew He would relish it; i knew The Man i Love. My care would be the heaven He'd never thought to seek.

Our defining moment would be perfect.

enjoy the middle
as much as you hope for the end
the best part of life happens there

There would be regrets. Lots of them. The morning skies would arise pale. The blue usually spread through its extension would no longer be the view—our view... my view. As the sunlight traveled to bathe the clouds we would all miss the blaze of pinks and reds. The beautiful life that lingered above our heads morning after morning would be gone. It would no longer be in existence. There would be nothing left. Nothing! No happiness for our skins. Light for our smiles. Flare for our hair. Absolutely nothing but an ill-fated smoke taking our strength away. Or, maybe just mine. i would look around and i'd see Him: The Man i Love. There would be much regret. i would be filled!

i wanted something painful. i didn't know exactly who i wanted to hurt, but i convinced myself that it wasn't Him. It couldn't have been Him. Mine was love to protect, to nurture, to honor; never to hurt. So, i couldn't honestly have wanted to hurt that man. Not Him. Not The Man i Love. However, there had been too many bruises, too many failed attempts at happiness, at hope. i had to heal somehow!

At one point in our existence, The Man i Love was who i was, or maybe just what i wanted—all i wanted. He was perfection, but He was also life. i still remember my dreams, our talks, His lies; i remember every single thing about our time. He was always there, even when He wasn't. Even when it was just me dreaming of a better version of life for both of us. The Man i Love was more than my reason for being. And, as such, He would have to be properly honored and verily celebrated.

For the sake of others, this would have to be done in a way that left no traces; that told no stories; most importantly, in a way that incriminated no soul; especially mine. i would have to erase any sign of my presence.

It was on me to erase the songs i'd sung while wrinkling our bed sheets, to wipe out every echo of my screams that clung to the walls like remnants of heat, like history hidden in the threads of our affair. All of it—I had to make it vanish. It was on me to ensure that nothing remained to tell the story, to speak of our secret passion, my despair, my rage. The Future could never be allowed to see what we'd done, to know that i'd lain bare, uninhibited, on those sheets. They could never know that my hairless, exposed body had pressed into the soft folds of those Cosy House Luxury sheets draped across the large divan— the same sheets now shading His still form. My warmth, sewn into every fiber, had to disappear. If they saw the outline of my contented, spent body in the fabric, they'd be quick to point fingers, to find blame. i had to get rid of it all.

For the sake of those who belonged to Him, i had to make sure our story was just that—ours, concealed from all others. They could never see the trail of my clothes scattered across the floor like fallen petals, nor could they understand the gravity of what had happened here. They could never know of my nakedness pressed against the countertop, an indelible mark left in the heat of our union. They could never know how He'd bent me over there, igniting every inch of me with an intensity i'd barely withstood, an intensity that left no room for regrets. They could never know that either.

It was on me to ensure that not a single trace remained.

i would make sure to use enough Clorox. Everyone would know of a different story.

With The Man i Love, i would always carry superior brightness, even when my wrinkles were outed. He was in the habit of spelling out His love. Giving it to me like i was a baby who couldn't have it all at once. He would look at me, fondle my face, and embed a kiss between my brows making me sprout a rainbow from my cheeks. It would be a while until the next one. Regardless of history, i know that He loved me like no one else. But, for Their sake, the story would be different.

i remember when The Man i love cracked a wall with my back. He wanted my pain to be His pleasing doing. That was true. He calmly pulled my box-braids and asked my flaming tongue to the dance of her life.

Despite the time grown between us; the lives that followed; even despite all of the other kisses i savored, it was Him, The Man I Love, who i felt gummed on my throat. The agitated stream in which i deepened, still washes away my mouth every time i bury my emotions with aching swallows.

The Man i Love was driven by His values, cautioned by His morals; inherently kind. He prided Himself in making good decisions, and He had always accounted for His bad ones. They knew that about Him as much as i did. It could still be true. They should've remembered Him that way.

i remember the very first time we met: we were both at a fundraising event. We exchanged words, but it's what we didn't say that got stuck. We gave each other one of those looks that shook ourselves to the core. i know how much He loved me. i felt how much He wanted me. But that could never be something they knew about. They would never understand. There would be regrets!

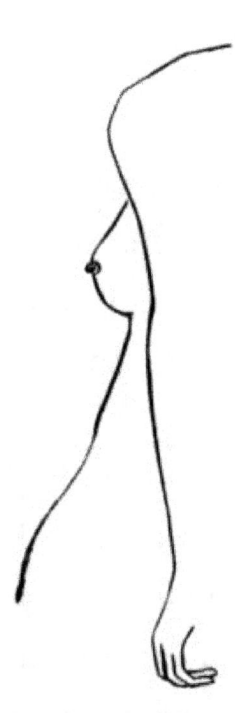

i would still be wearing my nakedness behind the extra-large spurious habit. The glow on His pupils would be a reflection of me mounting His manhood over blaring screams and lustful groans. The Man i Love would have me completely—'finally!', i imagined that's what He would think.

My left arm over my head. My hand holding on to my braids as though i would otherwise fall. The Man i Love would feel me. And, He would love it too.

He wouldn't know it then, but placing my right hand over the left side of His breastbone would be my way of showing how much i cared for Him. i would want to know exactly when to reduce pace and eventually stop. i'd watch His smile. i convinced myself that it would fade as soon as He started feeling His insides aching and shutting down. Perhaps a tear would be my cue. Sometimes, The Man i Love struggled with showing affection, but He loved me too much to hide His disbelief over the way He'd be meeting His creator. The timing, too. So, a tear, a forceful grab, a sudden move; The Man i Love would let know of His discomposure. And, as well as i have always done it, i would care for Him. i would care for The Man i Love.

"Do you like it?" — That would be a question to which we'd both know the answer. Still, seeing a "yes" slowly making its way out of His mouth would be just the boost.

"I love it!" The Man i Love would declare, with tone abounding in honesty. A smile would affirm the nicety of my actions.

The Man i Love would have His thumb involved in a slow dance at the tip of my lady. His hand on the back of my waist would be just the support He'd need to help me reach my peak and mark the moment for both of us.

"Clarissa..."

"Yes... do say my name."

"No.. Cla—"

"Shhhhhhh... just enjoy."

The bane would have made its way to His core. i would know it. The Man i Love would be trying to figure out. In any event, slow or not, i would make sure He had a chance to flood my insides. Our defining moment would be perfect. For both of us.

Still sitting my nuts on His screws i'd show Him another side of Mother. A dance. A slow one. Even with Trey Songz filling up the room with "Last Time," i would find a way to go as slow as a good Tarraxinha dance required. i would make sure my cheeks were all over His lower region. i'd mark my territory before it was no longer. At a snail's pace, The Man i Love would get to know me. i would be all over His southern region.

The Man i Love would look at me, fondle my face, and embed a kiss between my brows making me sprout a rainbow from my cheeks. A tear-filled smile would emerge, igniting the cunning mountains of His glorious round face, with no regard to the morrow. Somewhen, the blissful expression He'd be wearing would dissipate like blazes.

A moment for all of our lifetimes!

The Man i Love would lock His eyes with mine, spreading them wide with ornamental doubts. The tears that didn't make it to the paleness of our bedsheets would find their way to His mouth, wetting the dryness of His hiccups. Deep inside, He would know that'd be the only clear liquid going to deplete the pain and delay the darkening of His tongue. He would quickly swallow His regret; but, it would be too late.

No matter how many times i scrubbed my back; how many new sponges i premiered in the rear of my body. Not even all the attempts at forgetting would matter. i would carry Him forever. The Man i Love would be the hand i felt at the rim of my waist. Digging deep holes of mute desperation. Writing His story on my chubbiness. Eternizing the anguish of His happiness; His sorriness over the blight of our long-awaited coition. The Man i Love would be the faded smile staring at me with overwhelming fear. The look of dried love. He would be an ending still to be understood. No matter how many times i told myself different bed-stories, The Man i Love would be the sole reason for the sweat on my pillow. Even with the stars entrancing the skies, my nights would be too long.

If i did this, The Man i Love would be a mark for all forevers.

"Is this Clarissa?"

The answer would not vacate my throat too quickly: A wave of chills overtakes my corse. My eyes go round like blasted hula-hoops. My mouth blinks with the strength of a confounded slug. The usual signs. With the question drilling my ear, my disquietude would become evident. i'd watch my wrist with considerable unease, hoping it wasn't that time yet.

"Excuse me?" my thunder would be dry.

"I am sorry for calling you this way. It's just that my son spoke to me about you so often that I thought nobody else could help me understand a few things about Him. About His days. His final ones"

She wouldn't even wait for my answer. It would be as if she knew for sure i was the one. And i would feel credence in Her words.

if revenge were an effective solution,
many would be things of the past

Fresh grass giving off its perfume to life's ambiance. Covering up our feet with their dancing tails. Keeping spices of vipers and sweets of maggots on the wet draping of a firm ground. i see myself standing there, facing her nature. Watching as we became completely immersed in a sunny and breezy embrace. The wrinkled blazes of pinks and reds would also be the beautiful face of our Mother. She would take over part of the skies as ordained by the Creator. Unveiling the beauty of yet another day with bursts of bright light at the apex of all the green. i don't know why, but i'd wake up with hope, wishing i could see the sunrise again and feel the warmth of home awning on my body.

My hair. This beautiful-luminous-and-strong strings that resemble the branches of an imbondeiro tree. Each of them, as alive as Mother's greens; a crown to inspire.

My Face. This beautiful-vast-surface that is as smooth as the sweetest black plum out there. In its entirety, flawless.

My neck. This long-and-juicy adorn mimicking that of Mother's tallest giraffes. Being the sexiest of them all. The pillar of my elegance, with His kisses planted all over.

My race. This enthralling covering, matching the grains of Lovina, plagiarizing its darkness. The only one to His liking.

My chest. This sky-warded breasts. Harden by His freezing touch. My polished nails affixed to His skin. A place for His rest.

My legs. These lengthened-radiant sticks. These two pretty and mighty engines. The cranes that take my beauty all around.

All of me. The life He ever wanted!

i knew nothing about this other woman—the transient tenant of His heart. i didn't know if she wore braids like mine, if her cheeks held that same enticing softness, or if delicate, rooked lines wrapped around her neck. i knew nothing! Perhaps she dressed in the same palette as me; on that point, i was almost certain. The Man i Love revered the hues of our gods, colors he held sacred. So, if she did the same, i could only guess it was because i knew Him well enough to see it coming. But that's all i knew about her, nothing more.

i didn't know if her breasts were lifted as proudly as mine or if her beauty held the same allure. But i knew, with a fierce certainty, that i was a treasure unmatched—a unique beauty, one he could find only in me. The long, radiant limbs i'd been blessed with could only frame my own charm. In me was everything The Man i Love had ever wanted.

i knew nothing of the game played over the phone, or how she came to be before the comforts of His screen. How she deceived Him, i did not know—though perhaps it was with that same shrill, unflattering voice that sliced the silence between us when she first spoke.

One thing i knew for sure: i had heard a female voice. Not as melodic as mine, but a female voice nonetheless. i knew nothing else. As i found myself deprived of proof, i decided to believe that was His sister's voice. And, she was merely being protective of the one we both loved. For a second it made sense. It worked. When it didn't, i understood she also had a debt to pay.

If i did it, hers would also be a slow exit. However, much painful; agonizing. i would give her days to repent. To look deep inside my eyes—with bloody tears running through hers—and apologize for ending my life. For attempting to take Mother's gift from me. i didn't know anything about her, but she would come to know that no measure of love would ever compel me to forgive betrayal. She would pay for all the pain she too caused me.

For all the calls that went unanswered. For the messages He didn't get a chance to reply. For the voicemails that never even reached His ears because of what i know she must've had done. For all the late calls i got because The Man i Love got distracted and forgot. For everything. She would pay for everything. Not her alone. But, she'd also pay.

The Man i Love would look at me, grab my face, bringing it closer to mine, and link our gaze. He would stare, filled with silence, until heavy drops ran down our faces. i would know exactly why and what would hurt. The Man i Love would remain clueless. The same would not be said about her. Just like i would understand my fell fate, she would hers.

i would never hold her responsible for my demise. No. Never that. The fault wasn't hers to bear. i am fair; i've always been. My judgment has always been sound, unclouded, and unwavering. The Man i Love knew this about me—He'd witnessed it countless times. i lost track of how often i offered Him forgiveness, the kind that cuts deeper because it is so freely given. More than anything, He knew i listened to the gods, that i carried their words like an ember, the brightest torch illuminating their commandments. The Man i Love knew this well, because He was the same way. That's why i knew He would understand.

"*Therefore, just as sin came into the world through one man, and death through sin, so death spread to all men because all sinned.*" The Man i Love had those words ingrained in Him. He'd sung them countless times. How many Sundays had He slipped into those loose suits, escorting His mother to church with a reverence that was almost holy?

Those words were etched into His soul. He knew their meaning. He'd understand why i had no other choice. She too would have to be put down. She was tainted now, a stain on the peace i so carefully protected. Her sin would bring her death, just as mine would bring my redemption.

"I never wanted this for you, but it had to be this way," i'd say, my voice as steady as stone, without a tear to dilute the moment. i knew nothing of her, and she knew nothing of me, yet in her final moments, she'd clutch at me like i were her salvation, her last fragile hope. "I don't understand..." she'd whisper, her voice a fading plea, a last breath wrapped in the soft tremor of disbelief.

"*You must be ready, for He comes at an unexpected hour,*" i'd think it but never say aloud. There would be no point. The Man i Love, however, would understand completely.

A kiss planted between your brows, with praise. The hair of my eyes interweaving, hugging each other, unconcerned about time. Your lashes would caress mine as we headed for a dissimilar buss. We would both be in the night. And, before any of us dared to blink, robbing her melanin, my lips would cease to imprint my love on the foremost part of your beauty. They would relocate with the aim of reaching the ones that were yours. Never rushing. Completely against skipping–no matter the scars. Marking all the sites along the way. Leaving silent kisses behind. Spraying smiles all over your face — the beautiful-vast-surface that's as smooth as the sweetest black plum out there. Then, arranged further bellow, reaching your lips, seeking a mouthwatering meeting, they would rest. On yours. My very own carrier of succulent delights, inside your court. With the hairs of our eyes still interlaced, you'd know how i loved you so. Beats would rush out of my chest at full tilt.

"I never wanted to hurt you. I hope you come to believe that," He'd cough out a plea.

The night's imminence would take its place in the time-line. We'd both feel the end of the day. The Man i Love would go through it twice. His throat would venture in to an offing coughing spree, hoping to suck me in.

"You have always deserved more than a shred like me. More than what I could ever give you," regret would be all over His face.

The Man i Love would begin to unfold His heart with swift, urgent words, His gaze on me as if we were back at that long-ago fundraising event. A rush of sentences would pour from His mouth, filling the air between us. Droplets from deep within His gullet would mist my face, yet it would be silence— charged and heavy—that would make both of us blush, just as it had the first time we met.

Our exchanged glances would stir something timeless, a connection that shook the very foundations of our souls. The Man i Love would open His heart, just as mine closed.

A look of painful realization would take over my expression, cascading like a downpour i couldn't hold back. i'd see the tears pooling in His eyes, the remorse that seeped through His skin, the guilt radiating from His pores. i'd understand it all. And for the first time, i'd feel the weight of my own foolishness—for seeing, for understanding, for so willingly accepting the absurdity of His obvious lies. Never had i so completely surrendered my own reason. But they say that, once inside, love becomes you, and maybe that was true. i just wished i knew when it would all end.

His eyes would hold the glow of nostalgia, and despite myself, i'd follow Him there. i'd let the delirium take over, stretching our final moments together, allowing us to linger in this fragile, fleeting illusion.

'Can I at least call you back?'

'That's what i just said... isn't it?'

'I'm only making sure,' He grumbled.

'Do as you well please. That's how you've always done things. i don't see any reason for you to act any differently now.'

'Clarissa—'

'i have to go.'

The last time we talked, it wasn't exactly courteous. My mouth was dry, my voice was deep, my time was... oh well, i seemed to have no time for Him. But, i know that last one was a choice. i was just impatient about His ways. So, as expected, He went all out to fix things.

The halls were as busy as always. The pimples on the wall were just as hard, dressed with see-through droplets from our exalted thermostat. Marks of dirty shoes through the floor. Hugs and kisses thrown to the air like love and african history were the best of all combinations. A typical day at the museum. Until it wasn't.

No blinding light gathered at the entrance, forcing everyone into a flying sleep. The door didn't dramatically open, causing a convulsion. No. The visitors were just going about their business. i didn't trip over a pile of books never meant to be read. No. Ours was nothing like those goofy movies. That's not how our story resumed.

The Man i Love new exactly how to, inconveniently, place His tall and wide figure before my eyes. In all sincerity, no other action could have brought me to this moment. i was over it. Everything. Alas, He decided He had to disguise as a knight in shining armor. As my knight in shining armor. i would be well withing my rights to set Him straight. He'd know i was no puppet.

"i was really hoping to find you here."

It looked like His eyes were actually charged with remorse. Like it was all true.

"Do you remember me?" i read His fear.

"How could i ever forget?" The Man I Love understood that they were questions that required no answers, no filled silences.

"Life quickly takes away the good things because they are not stains. The bad stays and becomes the death of all days. So, yes, i remember you. What I can't explain is what you are doing here."

"Is everything okay here?" Frank asked. Even from far away, He saw my resentment.

"I thought this would be better than an overdue call-back. I—"

The Man i Love saw the madness that stripped me down of the glossy lipstick i was wearing. The unruffled nod i gave Frank was not meant for Him too, He understood that.

"Why stop now? You seem to have an agenda. I suggest you go along with it. You may never get another change."

That's when i realized what i had to do.

"Clarissa, you're angry. I understand. And you're right, I came here wanting to say things. But now..." — yet another awkward silence briskly grow between us. But before i could share my rush, The Man i Love added to His deliverance — "...now, i just want a chance at a dinner and a proper conversation with you. You think you can grant me that?"

Don't know what crossed my mind at that moment, but i gave Him an answer before i went to meet Frank.

tell yourself the same lie enough times
and it'll become the deed that chimes

When we met, He smiled. The tilted ground between us allowed me to see His perfect vertical measurements. His posture was striking. It looked as if He was able to reach the highest of skies. And, His smile was just as snowy as the cleanest clouds. He looked at me and, He smiled. Even from far away, overcrowded by blinding winds. The Man i Love smiled. Pain was all around. We were literally surrounded by broken hearts and vanished hopes, and yet He smiled. The Man i Love smiled. That's all it took. i believed life could be more. i felt it on my bones. It broke out from my pores. The biggest sign was the itch between my legs. The anticipation along my thighs was very intense.

He loved me.

When He spread out His smile for the sake of distracting mine. When He made our blazing looks intertwine; even though He had another on His field of view, His love for me was true. i was there, in the innermost part of His body. Beating, with all its might, like a really good rap song. For The Man i Love, i was more than residue. This i knew. He loved me. In the mornings, when His heart sung, it was my name at its pace. Each breath would be a silent declaration. 'I love you,' He would say. No one else would hear it. No one else could. No one but me. When sunlight set fire to the window of His soul, my face—this beautiful-vast-surface that is as smooth as the sweetest black plum out there—would be its most prominent feature. No even the strength of a starless night could conceal my existence, for i have always been there, in the apple of His eyes. The Man i Love also loved me, a lot.

He wanted me.

When He ousted lies, in the eve of yet another goodbye. Just before i gathered strength to let time take Him away, The Man i Love came to sway: 'If you must know, I have been thinking about the fact—the sad fact, i should add—that we haven't really talked in a while and... that... we most definitely should. And... I've also been thinking about how much I've missed you. And, that i should've just called.' This was Him—The Man i Love—suspiciously offering promises, like a houseowner offers cheese to a mouse. Every time i tried to be happy, He would be there. He would look at me, He would smile, He would use the most beautiful words in the dictionary to let me know just how much He wanted me. Not even a lie of my own would convince Him to let me go. He would make it seem like everything that ever twisted my mind was in fact the deepest truth.

He spoiled me.

When He planted the most earsplitting kiss in the mountains of my face. When He forced a smile out of my rage with the light of His eyes. When that was goodbye, He spoiled me. With the rise of another day, i'd change too. i'd believe my night was gone and, perhaps, a new day would also shower me with blissful rays; however, it would be The Man i Love. He'd spoil me. When He spoke with one foot out the door—not staying, not going—His body would be neither here nor there. i'd be left with a glimmer of a smile and guidance for the meanwhile, expected to just be. The Man i Love spoiled me. When He returned the calls already out of my mind, long expelled from my worries. When He apologized for cuts no longer hurting, reopening them with no mercy. When i found myself locked in His warmth, taken like the one that belongs, that was Him spoiling me.

The Man i Love had my answer. Against my better judgement, i would meet with Him. i would give into His deceit. i'd be what He needed me to be. i would know nothing. He wanted that. The Man i Love wanted me unaware, overtaken by smoke and mirrors. At the end, He would have it all; He'd have Me!

Covered by a night under a polyamorous moon, shining down on all her lovers, we would stand at the edge of vast waves, swept up in the first kiss. Darkness would blanket the world around us, the ocean humming with its own secret life. Chills would ripple over her soft, rounded form, passing from her to me, spreading in electric waves. i would hold her closer, feeling the warmth between us battling the cool night air, as if nothing else existed but our shared pulse under the moon's watchful gaze.

"You cold?" The Man i Love would ask. Already with His jacked over my shoulders.

The white of the night's eye would be on top of those waves, exposing marks we'd both see anew. A kiss with a smile would emerge.

"Still thoughtful, I see. Thank you!"
"And you... still the most..."

He wouldn't know, but i'd be trading kisses for His silence. For less of His lies. i wouldn't want any stains on our last day.

The sky would feel closer than ever, with the white spread all over the seaway. The Man i Love would look at me, fondle my face, and embed a kiss between my brows making me set off outbursts from my cheeks. The light would be excitement.

"Should we get in?"
"It's just the cold or something else?" The Man i Love took every chance He got to tease me and did double or triple of the expected. Then, it wouldn't be so different.

Finally, as we walked away from the cold and stepped into the cabin we found on one of those apps, i would see the moment to embrace our free-will. i would stop stargazing and He would quickly go for the embrace that transferred His deepest desire on to me.

"I adore touching what's mine," He'd declare again. — Another wave of chills would unveil my frailness. — "Now that you are mine, I intend to touch every inch of you."

"When will you show me?!" The Man i Love would know the answer to my question had to be more than mere words. He wouldn't use another one; however, His hand behind my neck would be a question i'd hear at its loudest. A jumbled kiss would be my consent.

"I need you." His voice would come out deeper. His eyes would enlarge. He's body would look shrunk. Just like the other times

He screamed wanting me; only this time, i would recognize the lies.

i would allow the bane to make its way to His core. i would want it. The Man i Love would try to figure out. But, all His efforts would be for nothing.

"All of a sudden I'm feeling weird."
"What do you mean? Should we stop?"
"Please, I never want you to stop."
Those words, and the smile that'd come with it, would be like a fuel to my fire.

Still grinding my hips against His, moving to the rhythms of old blues. i'd show The Man i Love things Mother taught me. My soft cheeks would rest over His lower half, then slowly shift to find sanctuary on His face. i'd dance for Him, slow as a whisper, covering His every surface, giving Him something to hold onto, something to draw His mind away from the weight of His pain, His worries.

even He who created
charged for His mercy
it may not be easy, but
if it hurts, it should end

Words would get stuck in His gullet, trying to find their way out. A killing knot would hug His passageway with the strength of a million-year nostalgia. The Man i Love would get Himself lost in an ocean of me. Each wave would be the sound of my voice filling His ear. The both of us, once again, involved in long telephonic exchanges. Sucking each other's juices in most succulent kisses. Marks of my body attached to His, like history written with lustful fingerprints. Winds of desperation would come out of His mouth like silent prayers do. The Man i Love would spell out my name with blinks of all His fears. For His misfortune, it'd already be too late.

His voice would go away like spring winds. Disappearing into the silence of His groans. Whatever my ears wouldn't feel, my body would hear. i would see it all over my extension, marks of the storm His mouth would have evoked. The Man i Love would look at me with dancing pupils. He'd drag His mind around all He'd see as possibilities. Even those He couldn't explain. He would stare into my eyes in hopes of finding answers. Anything to explain the inflowing end.

The hands once on the dimples of my waist, would escape to His throat. His completion would quickly turn against Him, exposing all the reds inside His body. He'd want me to say something, anything. However, we would both know there'd be nothing else left.

"Do... you...?" He'd insist.

"What is it, luv?" i would know the answer, but never would i dare pain Him so.

Tears would gather at the corners of my eyes, but i'd blink them back, refusing to let them fall. i'd smile, giving Him a glimpse of peace to carry with Him. i wanted His last memory of me to be calm, unwavering, even if it was the hardest lie i'd ever told with my face.

My cheeks would still be planted on His bolt. Deep inside the length of His thread. The pain overtaking His body, i would feel inside of me. And, as He tossed His blooded air at my face, i would then look at Him, fondle His face, and embed a kiss between His brows, making Him shine all over.

i would stay. i would dance until He could no longer feel me. Until He could no longer be. Both my hands would go for the last of His warmth. The Man i Love would be loved like He never thought possible. Like a flowery breeze in late spring, i would crowd the grounds of His expressions. In the grace of my hands He'd find peace even before death came. i would nurse Him 'til His eyes closed.

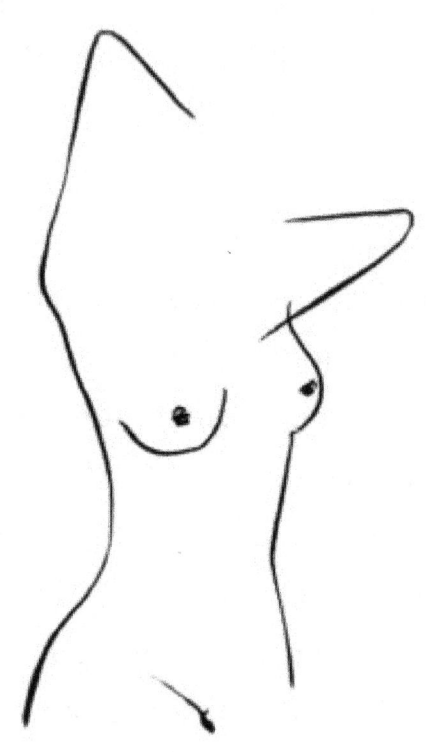

The sky would wear its blinding, shimmering light like a heartbeat, alive with its own brilliance. The night would be beautiful, and i'd have chosen it well—a perfect night. The heavens would dance with colors so vivid they'd etch themselves into memory. But by the end, only i would be left to savor the sight.

As soon as His hands slipped over my delicately bare silhouette, i'd steel myself for the final goodbye, allowing the lingering warmth of His touch to melt into the coldness that would soon replace it. Not a single word would pass between us that night. i wouldn't dare risk leaving pieces of myself scattered across that room. Slowly, i'd unwind from Him, pressing my palms into His chest one last time, leaving faint prints on His skin. i'd lift His head, gently placing it onto a pillow, maybe two, and stretch His legs, making sure each limb was set just right, as if for a long, restful sleep i'd want nothing more than to gift Him a final, chilling bath, to shield Him from what lay ahead. But the strength would drain from me, leaving only a heavy gaze lingering over His still form. i'd step back, fetch a fresh blanket from the closet—the color of untouched snow, as pure as my intentions. There was no hue He adored more, no feature He cherished more. i knew The Man i Love. i knew Him deeply. And that truth about Him would shape this final act. i'd wrap Him tightly, neck to toe, tilting His head to the side, as though He were lost in a peaceful dream.

Before i left, i'd make sure the house was beautiful, as serene and spotless as the home of a man preparing his own end. A place that looked like a palace, radiating a quiet dignity that would leave no room for surprise.

The cold that forced us together like magnets all night would be long gone. i would feel the day's glow approaching. Angry like never before. Like it knew all of my misdeeds.

No matter the sun's displeasure, i would honor that man—the Man i Love. i could never leave without ensuring everything was perfectly in place. i'd wash the dishes while His clothes spun in the washing machine, each piece cared for, including the shirts that hugged His arms, accentuating those strong muscles i adored. i'd clear out every leftover, every trace of us. Nothing could remain to tell the tale. i would never take that risk, not even for Him. Yes, i loved Him with all i had, but by then, what remained of me was mine alone.

i couldn't predict how long it would take for them to find Him, so i'd leave nothing to chance. i'd fill every corner of that space with a mist of Febreze, covering any lingering whispers of our time together. i'd turn off the music, leaving the air still, and plant a final kiss, one last goodbye, deep within both His dimples.

hard moments
may be turned into
bridges to better times

The high fires of the dew summer mornings would be quick to align with the midday sun heat. Their union would be long and their passion a feeling of echoing death. When the day-star would finally escape my misery, the clouds would resemble the strength of my cries. Never, in an ocean of eternities, could i understand the qualm of a heart that only gave love. But the mighty rains would show me. i would see it. Maybe i would never understand. But i would see it. i would see all the harm. Come the end of another long pouring and grayish day, i would cry like the fool i was. Like a lover ready to forgive regardless of the profoundness of her wounds.

i would slenderize my body just by pulling out my tears. Never my heart felt so gaudily blue. In the universe of all human pains, there would be no other to which i could compare. i would just have to feel it. Nothing, in my existence, would be harder.

No day would just be a day. The plangent chords of the perching birds would no longer be the beautifully happy wake-up call it always was. They would feel like guitar strings left tight around my neck, morning after morning. Each sunray would be a sward gored deep into my heart. The Man i Love would be everything. He would be everywhere. The winds of a late afternoon dancing on my face would be His touch, once again, just below my eyes. Leaving bubbles all over my extension. Little keen knobs on my entirety, reminding me of all you ever meant.

It would be the hardest thing to endure.

His mother. The lady of whom He always spoke so fondly. The human being that loved Him with her own life. This i knew. i knew The Man i Love. And, He told me so.

That unwrinkled woman always dying her hair brown. Not as tall as The Man i Love, but tall nonetheless. He would always have the biggest smile spread across His face whenever He included me in their memories.

It wouldn't be hard to anticipate her wide-and-bright smile. To see it slowly shutting down. To feel that all the energy of which He spoke, quickly dry up. Being wasted by all the pointless screaming.

The Man i Love spoke to me of Her kindness. Of all the love He had for her last born. He spoke to me of how much she loved spoiling Him, even with the stature of a grown man. i knew His mother loved Him as much as i did. Perhaps more. It would be the hardest thing for her to endure. But, she'd have to.

The Man i Love often said she was like me. Her care for Him, he'd say, was beyond words. And if there was anything i knew about myself, anything that reflected in His mother, it was the fight she'd have in her. The need to understand. The unyielding desire to reach Him, even now. But i'd reassure myself on one point: she'd never reach Him. i wouldn't allow it. i'd be the final link, the last line drawn between Him and anyone else. That much, at least, i'd control.

"I'm sorry to call you like this," she'd say, her voice trembling with a quiet urgency. "It's just that my son spoke of you often... i thought no one else could help me grasp this."

"I don't understand," i would say, though i'd have known exactly what she meant from her very first breath. But i'd never let her know that. Instead, i'd let the silence hang, leaving her to wonder if i was truly as close to Him as she'd been told.

She was the type to confront life. He told me so. She could dare confront me. i could clearly see Her at the museum's front door screaming my name and spreading false tales. From all i heard about her, from her own son, i knew i had to be careful about what i say. Beware of any triggers. i would have to make sure she had no reason to look at me sideways. Nothing that ruined the memory of their conversations. Nothing that rendered The Man i Love a liar. She would forever know me as the only one her son ever loved. i wouldn't care to stain that memory.

"Hmm, C, you look different."

i would want nothing less than to hear the nickname He made-up for me come out of the mouth of another. Not even Frank's.

"What do you mean?"

"Don't know yet. Just something about you. Is there something you have to tell me?"

"My Love, no idea what you mean."

"You call me My Love when you have something to hide. Are you forgetting that i know you? Why don't you just tell me?"

Sometimes i think Frank knows me better than i know myself. i should have realized. That was a poorly calculated move.

A bright-eyed smile was released from my face. Frank loved that about me. He loved to look at me and see the blinding light discharged from my pores. i used that against Him. A radiant smile was enough to distract Frank for a short period of time. i knew that eventually he would insist in pushing words out of my mouth. That would be just fine. i would be ready, but, as it was, i needed time.

"Frank,—" i smiled again. He got it then. — "I have nothing to tell you, nothing at all."

The gray clouds would bathe the sky with no mercy. Leaving no opening for light. At the outspread above our heads, we would have no light to cheer our skins. No opening between the clouds to let the rays kill us once more. No soul would be spared. We'd all feel!

Although we wouldn't dare say a word out loud, we would see the anger covering the extension that was azure-white once before. The flowers sitting above His grave would wither away, garnishing death with more death. The Man I Love would finally see.

He would never know the extent of my love. He would never get to understand its reach. Mine for Him was something much bigger. And, for some ill-luck He wouldn't understand. However, He would see. The Man i Love would know of the ember burning inside my heart. Whether screaming in agony bellow my feet or smiling above my braids, He'd finally see all i've ever carried for Him.

Despite being a good and delicate man—a caring man—T was a past i had decided to leave there. Phil, on the other hand, was only someone i once knew. Meanwhile, Matthew was undoubtedly a commendable odyssey. The most haunting memory i ever had. He was one of those guys to whom i'd never allot a second glance, despite the glasses, which, i admit, showed some kindness to his beauty. He wasn't tall enough—not as tall as The Man i Love, not even as tall as T. He wasn't high in stature, cloaked with savory meat, very-well built; that wasn't him. Still, for my maze, it was him who riled me up. i would go to Him.

My mind would drown in memories of her own. My heart would meet its hell. A place love was one face; one name. My affliction would cut me into pieces and His absence, then permanent, would be too strong a memory for me to bare sober. i would give myself to Matthew, He'd know to blast me.

| *it's not about how much you cry* |
| *but how much you smile afterward* |

The sharp beams of late mornings would quickly turn into somber nights. Flowers would smell of rue before they died. Heaven would never reach us. There'd be no songs from mockingbirds to embellish the out-most-sphere. It would be as if their throats were tied-up, cut-off; or put- down before the sun came up. No melody for life. My heart would hung as heavy as the moon in starless nights. The furthermost part of our history would near, never escaping my notice. i would face it with the same grace with which i've always faced life. Never have i feared the end. i carry an understanding that, eventually, we are all taken. The question is what we stood for while we lingered around.

i would be days into the grieving period. The time passed since the last instance His voice rifled mine would be long. Impossible to count. Unbearable to remember. Much effective to ever be forgotten. But for all that, my pain would feel newly attained. Still i would rise. i would face the beginning with the strength of a butterfly that just emerged.

Refined lines would settle under my eyes. Showing a feeling the world missed for the longest time. A feeling i missed. Maybe His mother would forever cry. Maybe she would allow Him into her dreams, night after night. Maybe His well-being would still be a concern of hers. But, i swear, it would not be mine. A smile would also be written on my lips. The widest i would ever see. i'd be happy.

The bone-chilling Tuesday would feel as promising as the nearing death of any Sunday. With the comfort of its chaotic winds, the clarity of her nights, i would allow myself to sense all of it. No other day would ever have felt as pleasant as that one. The night before would have the stain of a hunting nightmare. Still i would rise. i'd face the beginning with the strength of a butterfly that just emerged.

My right foot would be the first to greet the ground, then my left. i would start doing things the right way. For the very first time in months, i would undress with the delight of a hungry nymph, with the fleetness of a full-blown woman, the impatience of an old man. i would undress my-self with the honesty of my deepest desires. i'd draw the white blouse off my upper bout as slow as a turtle guards its own head. i would mess up my hair, more than the wind ever could in a night the windows were spread out. The bed would get another dose of my perfume early in the morning. It would be right there and then that i would start taking care of myself. Even before i got up to open the clunky curtains.

My right palm would drift slowly down to my knees, open and ready. That's where it would begin. i'd let my fingers trace along the length of my bronzed legs, moving purposefully toward the threshold of my most sacred self, with neither hesitation nor remorse, no intention of turning back.

i've lost count of how many times our conversations veered toward the provocative after i'd mention my state of undress. The Man i Love was endlessly intrigued by my nightly ritual of greeting the dark in nothing but my own skin. i loved that freedom, and He loved that about me. So i'd reach my lower curves with the same burn that lived within Him. Before the ritual of rubbing and groaning commenced, i'd take my bath gel, open the door ahead, and step into that little room with the bathtub we never used together. It would be there that i'd cleanse myself, washing away sin with the same eager fingers that moments ago had been instruments of indulgence.

i wouldn't try to understand it—this strange joy that flickered in the midst of my despair. i wouldn't waste a second analyzing its roots. i'd simply savor it, letting go of smiles as if they were scraps of starlight, feeling the radiance in my own eyes, something rare and unrestrained. i'd freeze time if only to admire the beauty staring back at me, to witness the gleam of a woman unashamed.

With water dripping over every inch of me, sliding along my skin in a cleansing caress, i'd renew every part of my land, every contour. The scent of sweet flowers would weave itself around me, spelling out my happiness. i'd slip into a dress bold as fire, long and flowing, the shade of a fierce orange sunset, my chosen armor for the day. A nude lipstick to match, five-inch heels to command the ground beneath me. Pharrell Williams would carry me to work, and i would be, for that moment, truly happy.

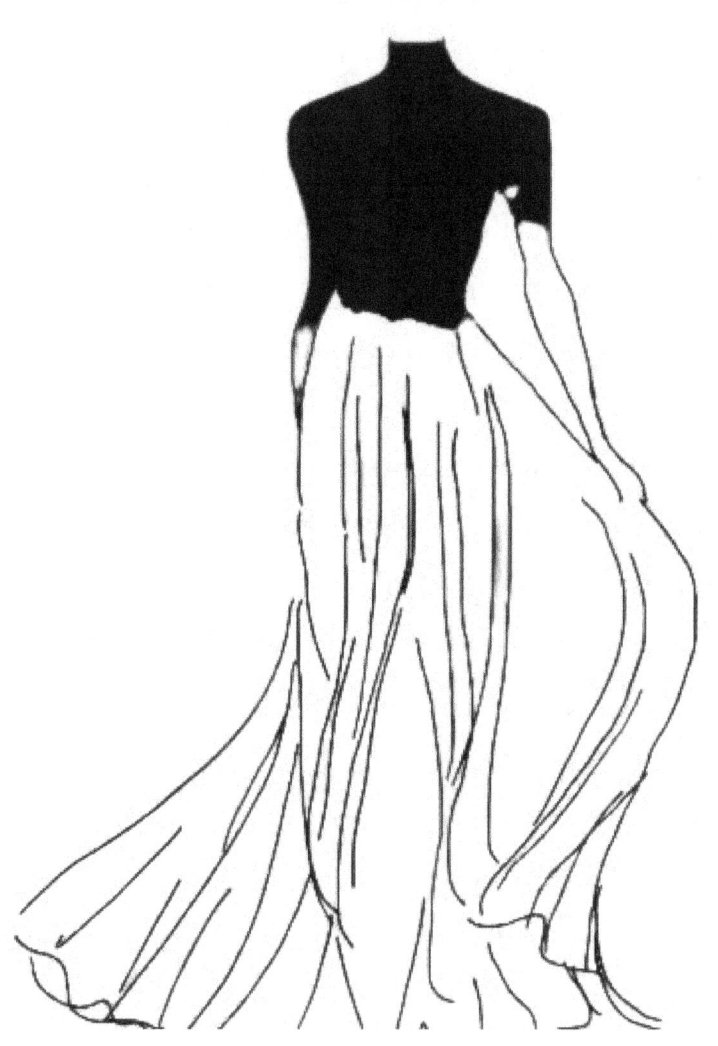

"Don't for a second believe you can fool me, cause you can't, little lady."

"What is it now, Frank? Can't a lady just be happy, dress up and enjoy a nice day?"

"My dearest friend, you know i love you. And... you know how much i need you to be happy for me to be happy, too. So, yes, you can and should always be happy—"

"I sense a but approaching," as i uttered those words, i hoped Frank hadn't felt my fright. Had not read my mind and seen my full-blooded darkness. i'd hope he had never met me. Not the person i'd tuned out to be.

"Yes, there's a but,—" Frank would say. — "I absolutely love this version of you. i just worry you're spending a lot of time touching the surface. You have to take care of yourself."

"You actually have no idea,—" that line would only be a thought around my head. i would never speak like that with Frank. — "you are right," i'd say. — "But, I'm taking care of myself, please don't worry," my words would come out as rehearsed as possible.

"I won't insist for now. However, know this, we will have this conversation later."

The frowns in Frank's face would be writings of his worry. He wouldn't be without reason to have them. i'd have given him too many of those with my quick-altering moods.

"Wow, Clarissa, you're killing it today."
"Yah, i gotta agree with Anne. You're the bomb, my friend," Frank's voice would be heard already a few paces away from us."
"Thank you... both of you."

i would be prepared to face another day. That day. My happiness would finally be my own. i would be the reason for my smile. However short. However bright. i would finally dress myself up with a selfish desire.

For the longest time He was my life. My whole existence. i'd go to bed with Him as an arranged dream. i would see no other face. i would wake up wanting nothing but His voice touching my skin with wet tongue. i would want to hear His perfume near me, like a song playing on repeat. My smile would be His. My tears would be everything threatening His peace. That was my life before our last meal.

i would still cry a few times. i would still need Frank's comforting hugs, his warm lap. i wouldn't be too quick to claim some sort of self-transcendence. That would take a while. Still, that's exactly the direction i would be heading. It would be my desire to trust Frank, but i would fear implicating my best friend.

Yes, i would adorn my figure with the most beautiful dresses. My feet would host the highest shoes. They would be my confidence. They would both be my happiness. No longer Him, the one I loved. No, that would be me.

In the fading light of a forced night, i spent my lunch hour behind a computer drenched in drool. Already away from my roused mind i found myself confronting my own reflection. The universe in front of me was the eternity of abstract seas protecting the screen. It was in the clarity of the waters that i was detained by my past, questioned by my present and spared by my future. Given an opportunity to, finally, write my own lines.

The fiery-orange-boldness disguised as a long-and-loosen dress was indeed my armor. The outer covering keeping me away from fear, self-doubt, and all that ever crippled me. The smell of sweet flowers spelled out my happiness. It was all the magnet i ever needed to find myself. In front of me, a reflection waved a forced good-bye while my hands remained kept under the dribbles. A voice, resounding like a dour snap woke me up.

"Who is it, Anne? Please, let them in."

"Wiisi – The Sun God", descanted on the voice of the deity herself — Wiyaala — was still pottering around the corners of the office like soothing whispers. i felt home. Suddenly, there was no place my mind wanted to go.

Confronting the hundred-foot glassy-wall behind me, lost in Mother's beauty, i was again alive. The traffic jam in the center of the city felt like the footprints i left in the sands of Mother. In the midst of my distractions, drawn in chanted truths, a shadow-like blast from the past emerged behind me, outshining my view. In the same breath years of pins and needles come rushing back. i insisted in believing the world was right, i was crazy.

"I think that's one of the most precious places there is," behind me, a voice i knew.

| *about the author* |

A soul with a multitude of vocations in perennial reinvention driven by a desire to ever incite positive change. The year was the seventh before the last of her century. Right at the beginning of the rainy season, under the far-famed Luanda's warmth, in the arms of a woman she also came call grandma, her first cries echoed, perhaps with no dreams yet. Solely remanded in an excessive attachment to her own interests. Nine dry seasons after that, on the eve of new rains, those high and rough screeches acclaimed the artist inherent to her. And, since then, she has also been that. Drifting in agitated yet compensating seas, with strong arms and now, steady aspirations.

"Writing is my life," she keeps saying. Cláudia has been writing for most of her existence. Her first book, Amores que nunca vivi was published seven (7) years ago. Many years after the first time she dared to eternalize her thoughts with a stroke of a pen. Since then, she has published seven (7) other tittles, both in Portuguese and in English: Pretérito Perfeito (2017), Cânticos de Apego (2018), Ahetu: Vozes Desprendidas (2018), Rogos ao Ímpeto (2019), Not for Floweres (2019), Amor, Sonetos?! (2020), and, the one you just read — The Man i Love Killed Me.

Apart from the above publications, in her literary repertoire, Cláudia's works are also published in a number of international journals, such as: The Red Jacket (U.S.A, 2014), The Sligo Journal (U.S.A, 2015), Best "New" African Poets Anthology (Cameroon, 2015-16), Antologia de Textos Premiados da AVL (Brazil, 2016), The Wagon Magazine (India, 2017), Teixeira de Pascoaes Vol.III -

Pensamento e Missão (Portugal, 2017), Antologia do Concurso Literário de Itaporanga (Brazil , 2017), Maryland's Best Emerging Poets (USA, 2018), , CIVICUS' State of Civil Society Report (South Africa, 2018), Empodere Magazine (Brazil, 2018), Philos Magazine (Brazil, 2018), Anthology of Portuguese Poetry "Entre o Sono e o Sonho" (Portugal, 2018), Quarentena – Memórias de um País Confinado (Portugal, 2020), and The VAW Journal – Voices of African Women (USA, 2020).

For Cláudia, writing is a direct link to people's hearts. It is a chance to have a true and reflective conversation in times of ever- ending dispatches. An opportunity to goad the world into action. Considering one of her biggest passions and field of study, writing is also one of the most impactful ways to teach.

Through life's storyline built with mistakes, eversions and effort, are signs of potential and gains from extreme devotion. In 2016, from Brazil, the Maria José Maldonado Literary Prize was the first I received. The following year, Portugal and Brazil honored me again with prizes for my participation in the Teixeira de Pascoaes Artistic Competition and the 6th Literary Contest of Itaporanga, respectively. In 2018 was the Honorable Mention in the 2nd Haicai Contest of Toledo - Kenzo Takemori. Considering the complexity and the multitude of the artist inherent in her, she live lives that continuously grant her reasons to thank and celebrate.

Cláudia Cassoma feels that the insatiable yearning to serve was in her even before she came to be. In an attempt to honor every single recognition, bring to life one of her greatest passions and, most importantly, answer her calling, she dedicates herself tirelessly in the creation and participation of projects that benefit the community around her. SmallPrints, Do Good Reading More and The

YA Project are some of such projects. And, driven by what she hopes to one day be able to contribute to the world, in early 2018, she participated in a training of historians — offered by the D.C. Oral History Collaborative, with the collaboration of Humanities D.C. and D.C. Public Libraries — acquiring certification and skills to effectively practice oral history.

Cláudia has been a mentor to the young and grown-up alike; an inspirational speaker, an editor, a songwriter, and few other things.

Today, still with errors, eversions and many efforts — always auspicious — she follows paths ranging from the art of graphic representation of language to those that bring the world closer to a hopeful metamorphosis.

| *literary repertoire* |

The Man I Love
KILLED ME

CLÁUDIA CASSOMA

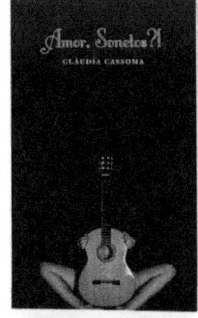

Amor, Sonetos A

CLÁUDIA CASSOMA

NOT FOR
FLOWERS

CLÁUDIA CASSOMA

Rogos ao Ímpeto

CLÁUDIA CASSOMA

AHETU
VOZES DESPRENDIDAS

CLÁUDIA CASSOMA

Cânticos de Apego

CLÁUDIA CASSOMA

CLÁUDIA CASSOMA

PRETÉRITO PERFEITO

amores
que ainda vivi

CLÁUDIA CASSOMA

| *your next read* |

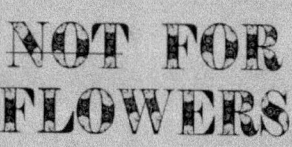

NOT FOR
FLOWERS

CLÁUDIA CASSOMA

In this compendium of earthshaking villanelles, readers are immersed into the boldest voices of fueled women. The puissant composition addresses a massive array of subjects, including: identity, friendship, solitude, life, death, courage, love, intimacy, femininity and defiance. Like a genuine healer, with each line, the speaker prescribes leveled self-esteem, self-confidence, self-reliance, self-fulfillment, a high dose of equality and more. Each verse form is a potential antidote for the myriad of human maladies, many self-inflicted due to wrongheaded preconceived notions. ~~NOT~~ FOR FLOWERS is reflection, warning, praise, and an unending celebration.

Read it!

FAÇA O BEM

DO GOOD READING MORE   **LENDO MAIS**

#CCDGRM
#CCDoGoodReadingMore

Contributing to social development is a passion I pursue with intensity, a responsibility I embrace with conviction, and a purpose I strive to honour through my work. DO **GOOD READING MORE** (faça o bem lendo mais) is one expression of that commitment: an initiative dedicated to promoting reading and supporting practices with social and community impact. As part of this mission, a percentage of the profits from my published books is devoted to causes that combat social inequality and contribute to building more just, inclusive, and compassionate communities.

Discover the difference your reading makes:

+Info: www.claudiacassoma.com/purpose